NEW in IDEAS CHESS

CARDOZA PUBLISHING

LARRY EVANS

Cardoza Publishing is the foremost gaming publisher in the world with a library of more than 200 up-to-date and easy-to-read books and strategies. These authoritative works are written by the top experts in their fields and with more than 10,000,000 books in print, represent the best-selling and most popular gaming books anywhere.

Library of Congress Catalog No: 2010941398
ISBN 10: 1-58042-274-8
ISBN: 13 978-1-58042-274-1

Visit our website or write us for a full list of our books, software and advanced strategies.

CARDOZA PUBLISHING
P.O. Box 98115, Las Vegas, NV 89193
Phone (800)577-WINS
email: cardozabooks@aol.com
www.cardozabooks.com

TABLE OF CONTENTS

ABOUT THE AUTHOR

Grandmaster Larry Evans, one of America's most celebrated chess authorities, is a five-time USA champion and author of more than 20 chess books including *New Ideas in Chess, Test Your Chess I.Q., Chess Endgame Quiz*, and a collaboration on Bobby Fischer's classic *My 60 Memorable Games.* He is a longtime contributor to *Chess Life*, and his syndicated chess column, *Evans On Chess*, has appeared continuously since 1971. Evans has beaten or drawn games against six world champions: Euwe, Karpov, Petrosian, Spassky, Smyslov, and Fischer, as well as dozens of the worlds' top players.

Evans first won the Marshall Club Championship at 15 and the New York State Championship at 16. He won the USA Closed Championship five times (the first time in 1951, the last time in 1980–a remarkable span), the USA Open four times, the 1956 Canadian Open, and many other opens including first place at an international tournament in Portugal 1974. Evans represented the USA on eight Olympic teams (including the gold medal team in 1976) and served as captain in 1982. Evans was the youngest player to capture the nation's highest chess title at age 19, a record surpassed by Bobby Fischer at 14. He is often referred to as the dean of American chess.

PREFACE

MY SYSTEM

The great thing about chess is that checkmate ends the game. And no lawyer can help.

Revisiting a book that I wrote over fifty years ago to convert it from descriptive to algebraic notation due to popular demand proved to be a daunting but enjoyable task. This time I had the benefit of chess computers, which were then virtually unknown but today are indispensable, to weed out mistakes and correct analysis. Thus this revision is considerably more accurate than the 1958 edition, yet despite the passage of time the basic principles outlined here are still valid and still guide my play.

The keynote of chemistry is that elements may combine to create new entities. The chessmaster is the chemist of a dimension geometrically bounded by 8 x 8. The elements he works with are Pawn Structure, Space, Force and Time. The amateur is vaguely aware these exist but doesn't always know how they interact or how to manipulate them properly. These elements, moreover, are so absolute that if chess is still played the same way a hundred years from now they will remain intact.

A famous principle of conservation in physics states that matter may be converted into energy and vice versa, but the total quantity of both together in a closed system remains unchanged. Since the chessboard is a closed system, these "new ideas" would lead us to suspect that an advantage in any one element may be converted into another element with proper technique. In general, the whole process of chess technique aims an converting the less durable into the more durable advantage. What is meant by an advantage and how to recognize it is the domain of this book. The purely tactical problem of how to exploit an advantage is dealt with in the illustrative examples, all taken from actual play.

Some masters are notoriously inarticulate when it comes to explaining their thoughts. When Bobby Fischer was asked how he improved so fast, he could only blurt out, "I just got good." As we collaborated on his *My 60 Memorable Games* I was pleasantly surprised (and flattered) to find that he had read this book avidly and absorbed its ideas. He told me that my games all looked like they came from the pages of this book. In his game 38 (Fischer-Keres, move 27) he noted: "Cashing in! Converting a spatial advantage into a material one (see Evans' *New Ideas In Chess)."*

Grandmasters can't always explain what they do or why they do it. They trust intuition and experience. "I hardly ever calculate the play in detail. I rely very much on an intuitive sense which tells me what are the right moves to look for," said Miguel Najdorf, Argentina's leading star for decades

Olaf Ulvestad, an American master of the 1940s, was asked to define the difference between a master and a grandmaster. "A master agonizes and sweats and grinds to find the best square for a knight," he said. "A grandmaster tosses a knight into the air and it lands on the best square." In other words, great chess is in the fingertips—just as Picasso avowed that his hand told his eye what to see.

This book came about because it dawned on me one morning to search through my games to see why I selected one move over another. What guided my hand? If I could explain it to myself, then surely I could explain it to others. I arrived at these principles by studying chess classics and by replaying all my tournament games to see why I won or lost, then extracted the quintessence from each one.

I can't claim to be the father of a system like Steinitz or Nimzovich. We all stand on the shoulders of these giants. What is "new" is my attempt to clearly define basic principles for players who want to improve. Arguably my chief contribution was to elevate Pawn Structure as a key element in the hallowed trinity of Force, Space and Time. These illustrations start with a snapshot of the critical moment (instead of the whole game) plus a headline of the principle involved in finding the best move. If necessary set up the position on your own board but try to work directly from the diagram to sharpen your visualization skills.

When this book came out chess computers were still in their infancy and we all considered them something of a joke. Nobody dreamed they would ever beat the world champion, let alone solve the game. Times are changed and now we are no match for machines which never tire and never make mistakes. But I believe chess will survive this silicon onslaught and continue to be enjoyed in clubs, parks and prisons. "Chess belongs to the ages," remarked Stefan Zweig in *The Royal Game.* "It slays boredom, sharpens the wits, and exhilarates the spirit."

Numerous books instruct us on how to win in the opening, how to win in the middle game, or how to win in the ending. But chess is a game of understanding, not memory, and as far as I know the only way to win is to outplay your opponent. My mission is to help you checkmate that guy on the other side of the board, and this book is designed to help you do just that.

Many players have told me that after reading this book their chess improved by leaps and bounds. I hope that you can say the same.

 # THE EVOLUTION OF CHESS

UNTIL MORPHY

"The beauty of a game is assessed, and not without good reason, according to the sacrifices it contains."—Rudolph Spielmann

Modern chess, in its infancy, abounded in brilliancies and swashbuckling combinations. Whatever players may have lacked, it was not imagination.

Oddly, leading masters rarely were the victims of their own tactics. Most of the 85 games of the six Labourdonnais-MacDonnell matches in 1834 were not noted for their brevity. Apparently lesser mortals seldom wondered why masters polished off amateurs in short, sparkling "parties" while their own battles against each other often lasted so long. Masters were possessed of a chess "daemon"—that was all there was to it—and they certainly did little to disturb this notion. Their knowledge was guarded jealously and imparted for fancy fees in private lessons.

What set masters apart was their grasp of "general principles." The value of Time and the importance of Force had always been recognized, though some people argued that odds of pawn and move are an advantage because they permit Black to develop a rapid attack along the semi-open f-file.

The essential difference from the 19th century is that the modern master who is confronted with a choice between a relatively transitory advantage in Time and a rather more permanent one in Space will generally choose Space. Confident in his defensive technique, he willingly submits to a short term evil for a long term good. Often this means accepting a difficult but tenable position in the hope of winning the endgame, if and when it can be reached. The early 19th century players did not have a deep insight into the real value of Time. Premature attacks were the rule and the same piece might be moved repeatedly in the opening, neglecting the harmonious development of the other pieces. The art of defense was in such disarray that inferior tactics often prevailed. It was not that players were obtuse—the leading masters of that era probably would excel today—but the basic principles of strategy, like the electric light, hadn't been invented yet.

The pioneers of modern chess were sharply rebuked for "taking the fun out of the game," a rage echoed a century later against machines. "My God! Why are computers trying to ruin chess? Maybe I should start to look for a second career," groused British GM Nigel Short in 1988.

The romantics were so enraptured with aesthetics that they almost felt cheated when sound defense frustrated a brilliancy. Were they oblivious to the satisfaction derived from a finely played lost game rather than from any number of wins derived from an opponent's errors? Someone might have been thought mad saying as Napier did after losing to Lasker at Cambridge Springs in 1904, "This is the finest game I ever played!"

Games where stodgy defense prevailed were seemingly devoid of beauty—for what beauty was there in grubby, materialistic, boring strategy? If that was all there was to chess, as well take up whist. Oldtimers wanted to witness games worthy of being showered with pieces of gold. They didn't seem to realize that if the standard of defense were raised it would inevitably raise the standard of attack.

Many of the so-called "immortal games" strike us today as downright ugly. We lose patience with the defender who forages with his queen for material gain while neglecting the development of his minor pieces. Most modern duffers could put up a better defense than the losers. Again, this is not meant to disparage players of a bygone era or to minimize the beauty of their conceptions, some of which have never been excelled, but solely to emphasize how much strategy has progressed since then.

"The beauty of a game is assessed, and not without good reason, according to the sacrifices it contains," observed Spielmann. Let's consider two celebrated examples—The Immortal Game and The Evergreen Partie. As with composed chess problems, we don't need to inquire just how such curious predicaments were reached. But if we diagram each position just before the final combination, it becomes a thing of beauty and a joy to behold! Needless to add, the brilliancy is often superfluous. In Diagram 1, for instance, the prosaic 22 Qxf7 wins just as handily as the flashy text.

"THE IMMORTAL GAME"
ANDERSSEN—KIESERITZKY

London 1851

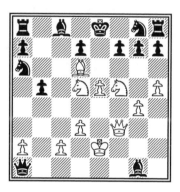

Diagram 1
White to play and win

21 Nxg7+ Kd8 22 Qf6+! Nxf6 23 Be7 mate.

"THE EVERGREEN PARTIE"
ANDERSSEN—DUFRESNE

Berlin 1852

Diagram 2
White to play and win

21 Qxd7+! Kxd7 22 Bf5+ Illustrates the power of the double check. **Ke8** Or 22...Kc6 23 Bd7 mate. **23 Bd7+ Kd8 24 Bxe7 mate.**

Clearly there are important differences between these two diagrams, but the similarities are meaningful. Black has moved his queen many times and is overwhelmingly ahead in material and both Black kings are still stranded in the center. The major difference is that in Diagram 1 most of Black's pieces are undeveloped (still on their original squares) whereas in Diagram 2 he has mobilized a formidable counterattack and actually threatens mate in one. This spiritual similarity is no accident and Anderssen, arguably the best of the pre-Morphyites, was on the winning side each time.

Along came Morphy (1837-1884) who toyed with Anderssen (1818-1879), who won the first great international tournament at London in 1851. After he got trounced in their 1858 match, Anderssen wrote: *"He who plays Morphy must abandon all hope of catching him in a trap, no matter how cunningly laid, but must assume that it is so clear to Morphy that there can be no question of a false step."*

Even this magnanimous tribute fails to credit Morphy's revolutionary new principles. Maybe Anderssen himself did not fully appreciate why he had lost! It is noteworthy that he displays a certain uneasiness by calling his own attacks merely "traps." Morphy's attacks, on the other hand, flowed organically out of the position while Anderssen's were more often an inspiration of the moment. Morphy knew not only how to attack, but also when—and that is why he won.

Morphy defeated everyone in sight. During his triumphant European tour in 1858 he sought in vain to arrange a match with England's Howard Staunton (1810-1874) a Shakespearean scholar and self-proclaimed world champion. Frustrated by Staunton's evasions, Morphy returned to New Orleans, then practiced law and abandoned chess entirely. For Freudians we recommend "The Problem of Paul Morphy" by Dr. Ernest Jones, which can be found in that excellent anthology *The Chess Reader* (1949). His legend still flourishes. *Paul Morphy,* a wonderful play by Noah Sheola, made its debut in 2006. Morphy was a child prodigy and Creole aristocrat fluent in four languages who ended his days as a paranoid recluse in the care of his mother and sister. The play examines his futile struggle to escape from the prison of his own phenomenal talent. *Paul Morphy: The Pride and Sorrow of Chess* by David Lawson (1976) is considered to be the definitive biography.

In an era when the dynamic young United States was suffering from a cultural inferiority complex, Morphy became a hero to millions of countrymen who didn't even play chess. He was glorified by the press as the first American representative to triumph over Old World culture. Europeans, loathe to admit than an outlander might possess a talisman unknown to them, awakened to the fact that maybe their masters had no "daemon" at all. Maybe there were certain principles which, once grasped, would enable anyone to rise as far as his ability permitted. The Royal Game became a little less royal. It became democratic.

PAUL MORPHY AND THE ROMANTICS: OPEN GAME

"Help your pieces so that they can help you." — Paul Morphy

In the late 18th century André Philidor (1726-1795) a distinguished composer as well as an excellent chessplayer (who, by the way, is mentioned in Rousseau's "Confessions") enunciated his great doctrine that *"the pawn is the soul of chess."* This implied that Pawn Structure, the most inert element, largely determines the character of the position and the plan appropriate to it (see Diagram 16 (p. 41)). In his games he showed how to assault an enemy fortress by using pawns as battering rams backed up by heavy pieces.

SMITH—PHILIDOR

London 1790

Diagram 3

Black's kingside pawns are battering rams. Notice how Black has massed both rooks behind his pawns. White's apparently impregnable king position has a weakness on g3. It requires but a few thrusts to demolish it entirely—against inferior defense.

1,,,h4?! Better is 1...Bc7. **2 Qf2?** Correct is 2 f4! gxf4 3 Ng4! snatching the initiative. **Bc7 3 Ne2 hxg3 4 Qxg3 Qxg3+ 5 Nxg3 Nf4+ 6 Kh1 Rxh3 7 Rg1 Rxh2+ 8 Kxh2 Rh8+ 9 Nh5 Rxh5+ 10 Kg3 Nh3+ 11 Kg4 Rh4 mate.**

This patient, closed game did not suit the temperament of Louis Charles LaBourdonnais (1797-1840). He perceived that slow, systematic massing of pawns did not apply to the opening which requires straightforward development in the center. He combatted every enemy unit with a force at least equal to it and rebuffed his foe with hand-to-hand fighting while seeking to establish a solid central outpost of his own.

LABOURDONNAIS—MACDONNELL

Match 1834

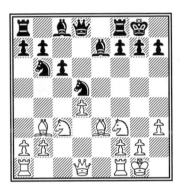

Diagram 4

White moves. Chances are equal in this very modern position chances and the struggle clearly is for control of the center.. White has an isolated pawn on d4 while Black maintains a stout blockade on d5. White must act quickly to develop middle game threats before Black succeeds in consolidating and reaching an ending where the pawn structure probably will favor him.

1 a4 A modern master might prefer Ne5 immediately. LaBourdonnais reasons that you have to give up something to get something. The text weakens the b4 square yet has an indirect bearing on the center because the threat of a5 helps to dislodge the blockade on d5. **a5 2 Ne5 Be6 3 Bc2** Setting sights on the kingside. **f5?** Closes the b1-h7 diagonal but creates a gruesome weakness on e6 and forever removes the possibility of f6 driving the knight from e5. 3...Bb4 putting pressure on the center and occupying the hole on b4 is a reasonable alternative. **4 Qe2 f4?** Black's lack of strategy is obvious. He should be defending with a move like Bf6 instead of attacking! **5 Bd2 Qe8 6 Rae1** Another strong developing move exerting even more pressure in the center. **Bf7 7 Qe4** The threat of mate wins a pawn.

g6 8 Bxf4 Nxf4 9 Qxf4 Bc4 10 Qh6 Bxf1 11 Bxg6! hxg6 12 Nxg6 Nf8 13 Qh8+ Kf7 14 Qh7+ Kf6 15 Nf4 Bd6 16 Re6+ Kg5 17 Qh6+ Kf5 18 g4 mate.

After LaBourdonnais' death a dry spell swept the chess world. It was Paul Morphy who revitalized the Romantic tradition. He didn't mass pawns in the opening as Philidor taught but instead pushed only a few center pawns in order to free his pieces and open lines for them, even if it became necessary to sacrifice a pawn or two in the process.

Morphy recognized that Time was more important than Force *in the opening.* His pieces invaded quickly, depriving his harassed opponent of methodical maneuvers. His flair and flexibility so irked his critics that they leveled an accusation at him which has since been leveled at almost every other great master (particularly Capablanca): an inclination to swap queens to gain a paltry pawn and then nurture it to victory in the end, no matter how long it took.

These were some of the characteristics of the open game at which Morphy excelled: some center pawns have been swapped, pieces command open lines and a central file usually has been ripped open. Openings arising from 1 e4 are more likely to lead to open lines than 1 d4 because it is easier to force d4 (after 1 e4) than to force e4 (after 1 d4). The reason is that d4 is originally protected by the queen behind it whereas e4 is not protected by the king. Queen Pawn games generally lead to closed positions while their King\Pawn counterparts generally lead to more lively play. The tendency of modern chess is away from gambits and open games which have been extensively analyzed.

Morphy was the first player to fully realize the imperative of speedy development. He expressed this in the simple phrase, *"Help your pieces so that they can help you."* He was often aided by the unnecessarily timid defensive moves of his opponents, or even by their unnecessarily aggressive forays as we saw in the previous example when Black played 4...f4.

MORPHY—AMATEUR

New Orleans 1858

Diagram 5

Black moves. Black is two pawns ahead and should prevail with proper defense. However, he fails to understand the demands of the position by keeping the lines closed with f6 and retreating the knight to g6 after White's inevitable f4 so as to observe the key square e5. White must be prevented at all costs from opening lines by f4 and e5. Instead Black helps solve the problem Morphy has thus far been unable to solve—how to open diagonals for his two bishops.

1...f5? An instructive error: (a) it opens the e-file (b) it opens the a2-g8 diagonal (c) it opens the a1-h8 diagonal. Morphy proceeds to seize these open lines with his next few moves. **2 f4 Nc6 3 Bc4+ Kh8 4 Bb2 Qe7?** Necessary was Qf6. **5 Rde1 Rf6?** Instead 5...Bd7 6 exf5 Qf6 still saves the day. But not 5...fxe4? 6 Rxe4 Qf6 7 Re8! Rxe8 8 Qxf6 gxf6 9 Bxf6 mate. **6 exf5 Qf8 7 Re8! Qxe8 8 Qxf6! Qe7 9 Qxg7+! Qxg7 10 f6**

1-0. Hopeless is 10...Qg8 11 f7+ Qg7 12 f8/Q mate. The only way to suffer a bit longer is 10...Qf7 111 Bxf7.

The 20th century neo-romantics like Tchigorin, Marshall and Spielmann carried Morphy's lessons of the open game almost to the point of absurdity. They tried to render Force subservient to aesthetics and too often overreached, lacking the ability to discriminate between the beautiful and the possible. The Romantics, in general, suffered from a reluctance to discipline their imagination.

The Romantic style was characteristic of the man loving action and quick success. The classical reaction was due chiefly to the character of someone disinterested in the glory of ready success, who strove instead for lasting values.

WILHELM STEINITZ AND THE CLASSICISTS: CLOSED GAME

"A win by an unsound combination, however showy, fills me with artistic horror."—Wilhelm Steinitz

Wilhelm Steinitz (1836-1900) was born in Prague and later became an American citizen. A chess philosopher who hungered for essences, he sought general laws and loathed exceptions. When he finally revolted against Romantic doctrines, the break was sharp and irrevocable.

Steinitz realized the necessity of evaluating a position and then acting on that evaluation. This objectivity forbade him from entering a speculative combination and then trusting to luck. It dawned on him that a master should not seek a winning combination unless he can first prove to himself that he holds an advantage.

Steinitz felt morally impelled to punish the crime when his opponent violated the objective demands of the position, He himself made no attempt to win in the early stages, as Morphy had done, because he was convinced it was possible only after his opponent had made an error, not before. So he sought small advantages out of the opening which gradually added up to one big explosive combination. In an age where playing to win from the very start was considered the only honorable course (which he did in his youth) such a doctrine received a scornful reception. Not surprisingly, many of his mature victories were begrudged.

In 1866 he wrested the title from Anderssen, who promptly conceded that Steinitz was even better than Morphy. Yet so bitter was the enmity against Steinitz that even after he held the world championship for 20 years a self-appointed committee of three amateurs claimed that "Morphy could have given Steinitz pawn and move." And a noted critic attributed Steinitz's two match victories over Zukertort to the fact that "Zukertort was not yet Zukertort in 1872" (the date of their first match) "and was no longer Zukertort in 1886" (the date of their second match). Anti-Semitism undoubtedly was the driving source behind these smears.

Steinitz held the title until 1894 when he was dethroned by Emanuel Lasker. During his reign he was so anxious to vanquish critics who scorned his system that his style became more provocative. He made unusual moves in order to provoke his adversaries into playing for a win and overreaching themselves when the position did not really justify such an attempt. Quite characteristically, he wrote: *"A win by an unsound combination, however showy, fills me with artistic horror. "*Victory, he perceived, is possible only after one side has erred. Make no errors, therefore, and never lose!

STEINITZ—GOLMAYO

Diagram 6

White moves. White is a pawn ahead but how many players would care to defend his position? He lags in development, his king is exposed in the and has forfeited the right to castle. Steinitz was so famous for taking a stroll with his king in the opening that this maneuver was known as the "Steinitzian king." Were it Black's move 1...Rhe8 would regain the pawn with a winning attack, but White can consolidate in the nick of time. **1 Ne1!** This curious retreat seems to take a vital piece out of play but it prepares d3, bolstering the pawn on e4 and releasing the bishop on c1. The knight can later return into play with Nf3 gaining a tempo by attacking the queen. **Nb4** To prevent 2 d3 because of Nxc2! 3 Nxc2 Qxd3+ etc. However this is merely a trap—what one of my students called "hope chess." **2 a3 Rhe8?!** Aiming for counterplay because retreating the knight is pointless. **3 axb4 Nxe4 4 Qf5+! Kb8 5 Nxe4 Rxe4+ 6 Kd1.** White withstood the attack and reached an endgame where his material advantage prevailed..

The question is why should a position which looks so bad at first glance contain so many hidden resources? The answer is White's pawn structure has no organic weaknesses. Black has a transitory edge in Time (superior development) which requires the utmost ingenuity to sustain, but White can't be prevented from consolidating with 1 Ne1! Thus Steinitz's theories approached Philidor's in that he recognized the elements of Force and Pawn Structure as enduring to the end. Steinitz's technique enabled him to convert Time and Space into these more durable elements.

His theories bore upon something much bigger than chess—namely, life itself, struggle, reason, mirrored on 64 squares. His theories could be further elaborated in two directions: philosophically or practically. Emanuel Lasker (1868-1941) followed the first road. *"I who vanquished Steinitz must see to it that his great achievement, his theories, should find justice, and I must avenge the wrongs he suffered,"* he stated. Siegbert Tarrasch (1862-1934) took the second road.

The mantle of classicism fell upon Tarrasch who both enriched and impoverished Steinitz's teachings by emphasizing the portion which appealed to his own temperament. For example, he preferred mobility plus a weakness (like most modern masters) to constricted positions without weaknesses. A medical doctor, he famously proclaimed that *"Cramped positions bear the germs of defeat."* Now his teachings are the stock in trade of every player from Grandmaster to Grandpatzer: occupy the center, forfity it, seek mobility and small advantages, always play with a plan.

Even today in the photos passed down to us one can sense the arrogance of this stiffly posed German doctor. That his dogmatism should irk the younger generation is not surprising. And that there should be a reaction against his starchy pedanticism seemed inevitable. It remained only for the younger masters to express it openly after World War 1.

RETI AND THE HYPERMODERNS: FLANK GAME

"The beauty of a move lies not in its appearance, but in the thought behind it."—Aaron Nimzovich

The hypermoderns were thoroughgoing iconoclasts, and it seems no accident that they rose to prominence after a World War that ravaged so many established values and conventions. They attacked their classical heritage on the grounds that no two chess positions are identical, that the so-called rules and general principles result in rote chess when applied indiscriminately. The two schools immediately clashed on a crucial matter: the center. The classicists argued that **occupation** was imperative. The hypermoderns countered that **control** was the real necessity and they sought openings which allowed opponents a free hand in the center, only to cripple it later with deft blows from the flanks.

Latvia's Aaron Nimzovich (1886-1935) was a profound chess thinker whose theories still influence generations of players. He settled in Denmark in 1922 and from a small rented room in Copenhagen penned his classic *My System*. His great antagonist Dr. Tarrasch wryly noted: *"Herr Nimzovich has a pronounced liking for ugly moves. His main strength lies in original, often bizarre maneuvers which are difficult to refute in practical play."*

Nimzovich could be equally pompous. *"Herr Tarrasch was himself not too familiar with the process of chess creativity. The beauty of a move lies not in its appearance, but in the thought behind it."* He introduced the "ugly" Nimzo-Indian Defense (**1 d4 Nf6 2 c4 e6 3 Nc3 Bb4**) where Black exerts pressure on the center by not occupying it with pawns. He also championed the eccentric **1 b3.** Nobody could accuse Nimzovich of false modesty and his abrasive, biting wit shines through his prose even in translation. In reading his notes today, one is struck by a number of wrong judgments and faulty suggestions. Yet he is always sparkling and provocative.

The insouciance of the hypermoderns was remarkable. Gyula Breyer (1893-1921) once began annotating a game by giving 1 e4 a question mark, accompanied by an infuriating comment: *"White's game is in its last throes."* Why? Well, he argued, 1 e4 does not actually develop a piece, it merely prepares development by opening lines. White also has committed himself irretrievably in the center by creating a target. There must be a way to attack this target, even to **provoke** White into advancing his pawns and creating more targets.

Alekhine's Defense filled this prescription: **1 e4 Nf6 2 e5 Nd5 3 c4 Nb6 4 d4.** Black's knight has been driven from pillar to post, but meanwhile White has made no developing moves with his pieces. On the contrary, he has occupied the center to his own detriment, flat-footed foe squaring away with his feet planted firmly in the center of the ring while Black bobs and weaves and jabs to his heart's content. At present, White is thought to maintain a slight advantage in Space and Time which offsets his weakness in Pawn Structure. The Black knight on b6 is misplaced and serves no function other than having provoked White's central pawn flurry.

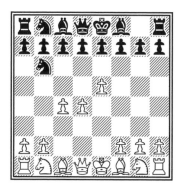

Diagram 7

White moves. Is White's center strong or weak? The "chase variation" puts the soundness of the defense to a severe test: **4...d6 5 f4** The Four Pawns Attack. A sober alternative is 5 Nf3 or 5 exd6. **dxe5 6 fxe5 Nc6 7 Be3** Timing is important. Not 7 Nf3? Bg4! exerting more pressure on d4. **Bf5 8 Nc3 e6 9 Nf3 Qd7 10 Be2 0-0-0 11 0-0** and White's center is still intact, serving its original function by cramping Black. The computer evaluates this position as equal, yet many masters distrust White's advanced center and the modern tendency is to omit 3 c4 and develop a piece instead: **1 e4 Nf6 2 e5 Nd5 3 d4 d6 4 Nf3 Bg4 5 Be2.** Or simply 4 exd6 instead of Nf3.

Since the opening is a struggle to dominate the center, hypermoderns sought a system that put direct pressure on it from the flank without fixing their own central pawns too soon. The ideal first move in such a system is **1 Nf3** which, moreover, does not commit the first player to any pawn advance.

The moves of the hypermoderns were not always new, though the ideas behind them were. *"The opening of the future"* **(1 Nf3 d5 2 c4)** as Tartakower dubbed the Reti—Zukertort system in 1924 (though Zukertort invariably followed up with 2 d4) had been played as far back as 1804 by Napoleon Bonaparte! The principles of the "chess cubists" were put to a grueling test at the New York International Tournament in 1924. Diagram 8 is a typical configuration of Richard Reti (1889-1929) who expounded his theories in *Modern Ideas In Chess* where he also railed against American "materialism" in chess.

TYPICAL RETI MIDDLE GAME

Diagram 8

Black moves. His pawns occupy the center while White exerts pressure on them from both flanks after placing his queen on a bizarre square. The computer evaluates the position as equal after **1...Ng6 2 Rfc1 Qe7.**

Eventually it became clear that the hypermoderns allowed their opponents too much leeway in the center. Their great contribution was in pointing out that an advantage in Space is frequently incompatible with an advantage in Pawn Structure. The school fell into some disrepute mainly because it failed to discriminate as it destroyed. It negated the best along with the worst of the classical heritage. There was, of course, an historical reason for their sweeping exaggeration. Classical theory was so entrenched that they had to overstate their case in order to be heard. By bending the stick to one side, they helped to place it in the middle. Their imperishable message is to keep our eyes open, avoid routine, approach each position with an open mind.

THE TECHNICIANS: NEO-CLASSICAL SCHOOL

"In the opening a master should play like a book, in the mid-game he should play like a magician, in the ending he should play like a machine."—Rudolph Spielmann

The technicians are what the word implies: they rely on technique and seldom try to force the issue or do anything contrary to the demands of the position. As a general rule Space is more important than Time which leads to settings requiring patience and endless maneuvering.

It is quite remarkable what a good technician can do once given the most miniscule advantage. Their emphasis often is on how to win a won game rather than on how to get one. Exploiting weak squares and accumulating invisible resources are matters of second nature.

Because of the slow jockeying for position so characteristic of their games, technicians are continually reproached with being dull and colorless. The average player is seldom equipped with the patience or the ability to appreciate this subtle brand of chess in which all the action seems to take place beneath the surface. Nothing seems to happen, no slam-bang attacks, no flim-flam, yet somehow technicians eke out victory. At Carlsbad 1929 Rubinstein extracted a win from such a hopelessly drawn rook and pawn ending that the editors of the tournament book united in the assertion that if it happened 300 years ago he would have been burned at the stake for being in league with evil spirits!

Great technicians include such illustrious figures as Capablanca, Flohr, Petrosian, Reshevsky, Rubinstein and Smyslov. They made few errors and lost few games. It goes without saying that they are very hard to beat. When they lose, it's usually in a manner that reflects credit on their opponents.

Technicians are generally content to hold their own with players of their own class while trouncing weaker players with monotonous regularity. The way to pick out technicians in scanning the crosstable of a tournament is to look for those players with the most draws against their peers. When asked whether he expected to win the U.S. Western Tournament in 1933, Reshevsky quipped: *"Who is there to beat me?"* Nobody did—but he didn't win the event. Too many draws.

In his book *Meet The Masters,* Euwe wrote: *"Reshevsky often wins with Black; there arise lively positions in which his tactical preparedness counts for a lot."* This is an apt observation. Technicians prefer counterattack and bare their claws only when provoked. They like ton let their opponents seize the initiative. The reason they draw with each other so frequently is that neither side is willing to take risks. Perhaps this style is not always held in such high esteem because the general public senses a lack of courage.

ECONOMY

"No second chance!" is the battle cry of the technicians. Economy—the execution of a given end in a minimum number of moves—is their trademark. They are masters of the finesse and the interpolation. Nothing escapes them, not the slightest transposition.

KRAMER—BISGUIER

New York 1955-56

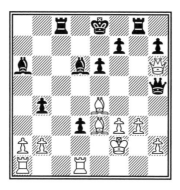

Diagram 9

Black moves. He must make White relinquish the blockade on e3 and the slightest transposition of moves can cost the precious initiative. The transition from this to the next diagram is accomplished by Bisguier without batting an eyelash, with a little help from Kramer.

1..Rc2+ 2 Rd2 Rxd2+ 3.Bxd2 Bc5+ 4 Kg2 Qxh6 5 Bxh6 f5 6 Bc6+? Loses. The computer found that 6 Rc1! holds the balance. **Ke7 7 Rd1 e5 8 Bd2 Kd6 9 Ba4 Bc4 10 Bb3 Bxb3 11 axb3 Kd5 12 Be1 e4 13 Bf2 Bxf2 14 Kxf2 Kd4**

Diagram 10

White Resigns. He is defenseless against e3+. Finally Black has conquered the vital e3 square and his onrushing passed pawns in the center are enough to make Columbus sorry he discovered America.

THE ECLECTICS

"Style? I have no style."—Anatoly Karpov

The eclectics inherited the Romantic tradition and fortified it with centuries of technique. They are primarily positional players who are courageous, original and sharp. While the technician steers for positions which are nearly always under his control, preferably keeping a draw in hand, the tactician surrenders himself to complications without being sure of the outcome or knowing where they will lead. While the technician strives for closed positions, eclectics like open games where things can hang by a hair.

The technician aims for the endgame, preferring positions that respond to technique rather than imagination. The tactician concentrates on opening theory, seeking new ways to launch a sharp and early battle, straddling the best of both worlds. A really strong player must be at home in any phase of the game, fully versed in positional nuances and tactical skirmishes. The difference is primarily one of temperament. Anatoly Karpov, for example, is famous for making unexpected retreats. He plays like a boa constrictor, slowly encircling and swallowing his opponent. When asked to describe his style, he quipped: *"Style? I have no style."*

If one could summarize the renaissance of Soviet chess in the 1940s it would be dynamism. (One wonders to what extent the values of a culture are reflected in its chess.) Leading exponents of the eclectic school mainly came from that geographical region: Alekhine, Bronstein, Geller, Karpov, Keres, Spassky, Tal and Botvinnik.

It goes without saying that the distinction between the various schools is not clear-cut or self-evident. Keres and Tal, for instance, switched to positional play when they no longer were successful with risky gambits. Tal was world champion for a year before his return match with Botvinnik in 1961. After falling behind, Tal rallied by winning the 8th game, then noted: *"Many people said 'at last Tal is beginning to play like Tal,' But that's not yet so. I've forgotten how Tal plays."* He then dropped three games in a row which allowed Botvinnik to regain the crown 13-8.

Symmetrical settings with balanced Pawn Structures usually are drawish. Eclectics seek double-edged moves to introduce imbalance by stamping a definite character on the game. This illustration is typical.

BISGUIER—EVANS

New York 1955-6

Diagram 11

Black moves. White threatens dxc5 capturing a pawn. The insipid 1...cxd4 2 cxd4 lets him free his c1 bishop and the position assumes a drawish nature because of the balanced ⌄

Pawn Structure. The game continued **1...c4! 2 Bc2 Re8 3 Bd2 Bc7 4 Ng3 b5 5 h3 a5** with advantage because Black has created a menacing queenside majority. Now White struggled in vain to get in e4 while Black fought to restrain it.

SHARPNESS

"Sharpness" means alertness plus precision. It is characterized by the relentless search for hidden resources and a disdain for the obvious move. Even if there are a hundred good reasons for rejecting a given move, the tactician is always ready to consider it and he often gains an advantage in this totally unexpected way.

"I can see combinations as well as Alekhine, but I cannot get into the same positions," sighed Spielmann. The next diagram is incredibly complicated, everything seems suspended in mid-air, Black's rook is *en prise,* yet the master magician Alekhine pulls all the strings. He finds one stroke after another, each more powerful than the last, so that his harassed opponent is given no breathing space. *"I think there is reason to nominate this game the most beautiful ever played in the history of chess,"* gushed Kasparov (whose own "immortal" victory over Topalov at Wijk aan Zee in 1999 also deserves to be nominated).

RETI—ALEKHINE

Baden-Baden 1925

Diagram 12

Black moves. **1...Nc3!** Counterattack, ignoring the endangered rook on e3. **2 Qxb7.** If. 2 Qc4 b5! forces the queen to relinquish its guard of e2. **Qxb7 3 Nxb7 Nxe2+ 4 Kh2.** Hopeless is 4 Kf1 Nxg3+ 5 fxg3 Bxf3 6 Bxf3 Rxf3+ 7 Kg2 Raa3.

Diagram 13

Now White looks safe because 4...Nxc1 5 fxe3 holds everything and looks drawish. How can Black sustain his initiative?

4...Ne4!! *"What a move! This new member of the cavalry will turn White's defense into dust. Now his best chance was 5 Rd8+ Rxd8 6 fxe3 although after 6...Rd5! Black wins the pawn while his pieces still dominate the board,"* noted Kasparov. **5 Rc4 Nxf2!** Even without queens the battle rages. The win of a pawn is not in itself sufficient to win but Black still has a fierce attack. **6 Bg2 Be6!** *"Black is clearly winning, but Alekhine's final combination makes this game a true masterpiece,"* enthused Kasparov. **7 Rcc2 Ng4+ 8 Kh3 Ne5+ 9 Kh2 Rxf3! 10 Rxe2 Ng4+ 11 Kh3 Ne3+ 12 Kh2 Nxc2 13 Bxf3 Nd4 14 Rf2 Nxf3+ 15 Rxf3 Bd5** snagging the knight on b7. 0-1.

ROSSOLIMO—EVANS

Hastings 1949-50

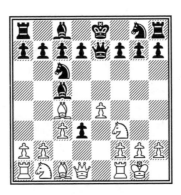

Diagram 14

White moves. An unimaginative player intent on repairing Force might play 1 Qxd3 giving Black time for d6 with free and easy development. If White is to sustain the initiative, he must first see to it that Black does not get his pieces out.

1 e5! This interpolation caught me by surprise. Black's game, though difficult, is still tenable. **h6** To prevent Bg5 but it loses time. The best practical chance is 2...d6. **2 b4 Bb6 3 a4 a5 4 Ba3.** I failed to find an adequate defense and for one of the few times in my career never got out of the opening alive after **4...axb4 5 cxb4 Nxb4 6 Qb3 Bc5 6 Nc3 Ra5?** The computer suggests the cool retreat 6...Qf8!—a defense most humans would never consider. **7 Bxb4 Bxb4 8 Nd5 Rxd5 9 Bxd5** gaining the Exchange.

PAWN STRUCTURE

In some primers, with good reason, endgames are taught first even though the novice seldom is made to comprehend why. "Pawn endings are to chess what putting is to golf," observed Purdy. More than this—Pawn Structure is to chess what cell structure is to life. After a dozen or so moves the master already is evaluating his endgame prospects. Should he try to simplify and swap pieces? Should he play to attack? Defend? Let's digress a bit—it's really germane—to see how this works.

THE OUTSIDE PASSED PAWN

Consider this basic principle of many king and pawn endings: "When there are no outside passed pawns, every effort must be made to create one."

If the Pawn Structure is completely balanced, it's not possible to create an outside passed pawn unless someone makes a mistake. That's why, for example, if each side has six pawns apiece, masters will generally make an attempt along the way to create 3 against 2 on the Queenside (see Queen side majority) and 3 against 4 on the kingside, rather than a straight 3 vs. 3 on each wing. The reason is that it's technically easier to create an outside passed pawn with 3 vs. 2 than with 4 vs. 3.

BREYER—NYHOM

Baden-Baden 1914

Diagram 15

Black moves. Here the forces are so reduced and the material so even that one is tempted perfunctorily to dismiss it as a draw. If anything, Black seems to have the more active king but keep your eye on that pesky outside passed pawn on c2. The principle involved is that Black must rush his king headlong in front of this pawn whereupon, at the right moment, White will pitch it and march his king to the kingside to gobble the remaining dark pawns. But Black overlooked a surprising defense.

1...g5! 2 c3+ Kc4? The drawing line is 2...Ke4!! 3 g4 e5 4 Ke2 Kf4! 5 Kf2 Ke4 6 Ke2 Kf4 and neither side can make progress.. **3 g4 Kd5 4 Kd3 Kc5 5 Ke4 1-0.**

PAWN STRUCTURE
DETERMINES STRATEGY

Armed with the previous example, let's consider the exchange variation of the Ruy Lopez after seven standard moves: **1 e4 e5 2 Nf3 Nc6 3 Bb5 a6.** The Morphy Defense which is still considered best. **4 Bxc6 dxc6 5 d4 exd4 6 Qxd4 Qxd4 7 Nxd4.**

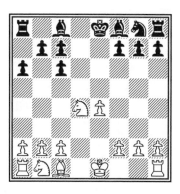

Diagram 16

White has a winning Pawn Structure but... This position contains many basic principles and many exceptions. For the nonce let us content ourselves with the following observations:

(a) In effect White is a pawn ahead on the kingside because Black's doubled c-pawns are worthless; his 4 pawns are held in check by White's 3 pawns. To satisfy yourself remove all the pieces from the board and try to force a queen against best play with one of Black's queenside pawns.

(b) As a result of his superior Pawn Structure White has a forced win in the endgame.

(c) Each swap brings White closer to victory.

This, then, is White's strategy—to swap pieces at each and every opportunity. The fly in the ointment is that chess is dynamic, not static. Black has compensation in other elements (the two bishops). "Before the ending the gods have placed the middle game," explained Tarrasch to describe positions like this where one side has a winning advantage in the ending *if he can ever get to it.* Mentally sweep all the pieces off the board.

Diagram 17

White has a won endgame and wins by creating a passed pawn on the kingside. There is no point in outlining the solution here. It may require dozens of moves, but that is a problem of technique. The process consists of creating a passed pawn on the kingside. Note only that if black's pawn were on d6 instead of c6 the ending would be a theoretical draw.

PAWN MOBILITY

Pawn mobility means the pawn's relative power to advance. Its unique ability to promote to a queen gave rise to the old maxim that "every pawn carries a baton in its haversack."

In our discussion of the outside passed pawn we saw that great power lay in its ability to advance unimpeded by enemy pawns in front of it or to either side. We thus can draw our first tentative conclusion: *Pawns that are free to advance are healthier than pawns that are unable to do so.* The point where every pawn has equal mobility exists only in the original structure.

Diagram 18

THE STARTING LINEUP

This is ideal because neither side has any weakness and every pawn is ready to offer fraternal support to its colleagues. The Hypermoderns were the first to fully comprehend the real value of this formation, but they went overboard in trying to keep it intact. Certain pawns, preferably in the center, must advance in order to get the pieces out and establish beachheads while the others stand guard as reserves. But remember—reserves can be called upon only once in every game because a pawn is the only unit that can never retreat. So push pawns sparingly.

Each time a pawn is advanced it either gains or loses mobility and crosses a metaphysical boundary that divided *essence* from *being*. The starting lineup is healthy because it possesses absolute mobility, absolute flexibility, absolute potential.

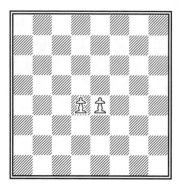

Diagram 19

MOBILE PAWNS

Mobile pawns are the most desirable formation. White's center pawns are free to advance without being hindered by enemy pawns on the same or adjacent files. They can be stopped only by a blockade with enemy pieces.

Diagram 20

SEMI-MOBILE PAWNS

Semi-mobile pawns are free to advance, but only relatively. As soon as they move, they lose their mobility. Thus if 1 e5 d5 locks the formation. So does 1 d5 e5 (or 1...exd5 2 exd5) and neither pawn can advance any further.

Diagram 21

IMMOBILE PAWNS

A pawn is immobile when it is physically unable to advance. For practical purposes pawns may also be considered immobile when they are free to advance but where doing so would cause their loss without any corresponding compensation.

TRY TO MOBILIZE CENTER PAWNS

EVANS—KASHDAN

U.S. Open Championship 1951

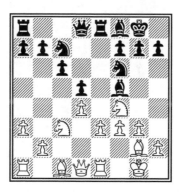

Diagram 22

White moves. Despite hypermodern dogma, occupation of the center more often than not also means control, especially when the center pawns are liquid. The time is ripe for 1 e4 even though it weakens the pawn on d4. White must open lines for his bishop on c1 and free his game. Note the elaborate measures each side has taken for and against e4.

The game continued **1 e4 dxe4 2 fxe4 Bg4 3 Qd3 Ne6 4 h3?** More prudent is 4 Nxe6. **Qxd4+ 5 Qxd4 Nxd4 6 hxg4 Nc2 7 g5 Bc5+** Stronger is 7...Ng4! 8 Bd2 Rad8. **8 Kf1 Ng4 9 Nd3 Bb6 10 Bf4 Rad8 11 Ke2 Nd4+ 12 Kd2 Nb3+ 13 Ke2** White wisely agreed to draw instead of 13 Kc2? Nxa1+ 14 Rxa1 Ne3+ 15 Bxe3 Bxe3.

PLAY FOR THE STEAMROLLER

EVANS—LARSEN

U.S. Open Championship 1949

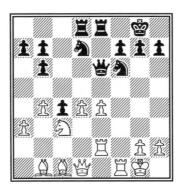

Diagram 23

Black moves. The "steamroller" consists of two or more connected pawns so highly mobile that one or the other is constantly threatening to advance, like molten lava. The best defense is to try and provoke one of the pawns so that a line of defense (or a blockade) can be established.

1...Ne5. In order to reach c6 and force the pawn to advance to d5 and set up a blockade on the dark squares (e5 and d6). **2 Bg5 Nc6 3 d5 Qe5 4 Bxf6 gxf6 5 Re3 Ne7 6 Rg3+ Kh8 7 Qf3 f5 8 Qh5 Rg8 9 Rh3 Qg7 10 Rf2 f4 11 Qh6** Leads to a won endgame because of Black's indefensible pawn on f4. But stronger is 11 e5! Ng6 12 Ne4. Black eventually lost after **11... Bc8 12 Qxg7+ Rxg7 13 Rhf3 Ng6 14 Rd2 f6 15 Rff2 Bd7 16 Ne2 f3 17 Rxf3 Nh4 18 Rf2,** etc. An instructive example of Pawn Structure converted into attack.

PAWN MAJORITIES MUST BE MOBILIZED

EVANS—ROSSOLIMO

Hollywood Open 1954

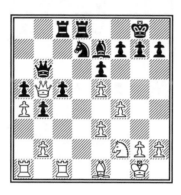

Diagram 24

Black moves. White intends b3 setting up a blockade on c4. Black can't permit this or his queenside majority (3 vs. 2) will be stopped cold. Note also that White is virtually a pawn down because of the doubled e-pawns.

1...c4! Timing is important. Black invites 2 Rxc4? Qxb5 gaining material but he avoided 1...Qxb5 2 axb5 c4? because of 3 Rxa5. **2 Qxb6 Nxb6 3 Kf1 h5.** White's doubled pawns are worthless and he lost. Black has a bind and it's only a question of time before he invades on the open d-file. White's rook must defend a4 and his other pieces are fatally ensnared.

SEMI-MOBILE CENTER PAWNS

EVANS—SANDRIN

U.S. Championship 1948

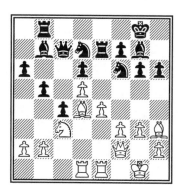

Diagram 25

White moves. His pawn on e4 looks immobile because advancing it apparently costs a pawn without any compensation. The real blockader is the pawn on d6. In order to mobilize his pawns White must demolish this blockade. But how?

1 e5!? dxe5? Of course not 1...Nxe5? 2 Bb6! snaring the queen. Also bad is 1...Ne8? 2 e6. White is okay after 1...Nxd5 2 Nxd5 Bxd5 3 exd6 Rxe1+ 4 Qxe1 Bxd4+ 5 Rxd4 Qxd6 6 Nxg6! Qb6! (if 6...fxg6 7 Rxd5! Qxd5 8 Be6+) 7 Ne7+ Kf8 8 Qf2. But the best defense is 1...Rxe5! 2 Bxe5 Nxe5 3 Bf1 b4 4 Ne4 Nxd5. **2 Ba7!** gaining the Exchange owing to the double threat of d6 and Bxb8. Caught by surprise, Black quickly crumbled after White mobilized his e-pawn. This often happens to cramped positions as soon as the lines are opened.

PASSED PAWNS

WHITE HAS A PASSED PAWN

A passed pawn has no enemy pawn either directly in front of or adjacent to it. It may be a source of strength or a source of weakness depending upon its mobility. In the endgame it acquires power because the queening path must be blocked by the opposing king, leaving its own king free for dirty work.

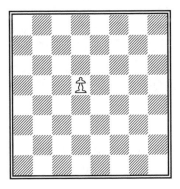

Diagram 26

WHITE HAS A PROTECTED PASSED PAWN ON D5

This is usually a strong formation.

Diagram 27

WHITE HAS A POTENTIAL PASSED PAWN

A pawn is potentially passed when the enemy pawn on an adjacent file can be cleared away by a simple exchange. Here White could create an actual passed pawn on d5 by playing 1 d5 exd5 2 exd5.

Diagram 28

PASSED PAWNS MUST BE PUSHED!

White moves. The passed pawn can be a mighty weapon even in the middle game if it is not blockaded and if it is backed up by major pieces. In short, a passed pawn which is also mobile constitutes a tangible advantage because when it is pushed far enough the enemy must sacrifice material to prevent it from queening. (See also diagram 32(p. 55).)

EVANS—R. BYRNE

New York 1951

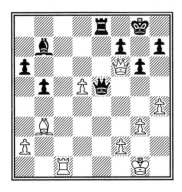

Diagram 29

1 Qxe5 Rxe5 2 d6! With the powerful threat of d7. Nimzovich indulged in a quaint pathetic fallacy when he attributed the onward movement of a passed pawn to its "lust to expand." **Re8.** Also hopeless is 2...Kf8 3 f4 Re3 4 Rc7. **3 d7 Rd8 4 Rc7 1-0.** Black must lose at least a bishop. If 4...Be4 5 Rc8 forces a new queen. Or 4...Rb8 5 Rxb7 Rxb7 6 d8/Q+.

CLEAR THE PATH: DEMOLISH BLOCKADES

EVANS—BISGUIER

U.S. Open Championship 1950

Diagram 30

Black moves. We have already determined that the strength of a passed pawn depends upon its mobility. Here the pawn on c2 apparently is immobile because of a staunch blockade on c1. White threatens 1 Nxd3 Bxd3+ 2 Kd2! hoping to draw with opposite colored bishops. Black must use his precious move to solve the problem by combinative means.

1...Ra8! Beware of Greeks bearing gifts! **2 Rxa8 Nxc1+ 3 Ke3**. Forced. Not 2 Kd2 Nxb3+ and the pawn queens. **Nd3.** Squelching any drawing chances arising from 3...Nxb3 4 Ba3 b4 5 Bb2 c1/Q+ 6 Bxc1 Nxc1 7 Rb8. **4 Ba3 b4 5 Bb2.** 4 Kd2 is refuted by Nc5!—a beautiful final point. **Nxb2 6 Kd2 Nd1 7 Ra4 Nc3** Inviting 8 Rxa4 c1/Q+ 9 Kxc1 Na2+ followed by Nxb4. **8 Ra1 Kh6 0-1.**

CREATE PROTECTED PASSED PAWNS

HOWARD—EVANS

New York 1950

Diagram 31

Black moves. A theoretical balance but black's Pawn Structure is bad. His d-pawns are doubled and his a-pawn is under fire. He must find some way to un-paralyze his pawns.

1...d3+! 2 cxd3. Disagreeably forced. If 2 Kxd3 Rf3+ followed by Rxg3. **b3.** Stopping this pawn from queening will cost White dearly. **3 Kd2 Kb4 4 Bb6 b2 5 Kc2 Ka3 6 Ne2 b1/Q+ 7 Kxb1 Rb7 8 Nc3 Rxb6+.** Having won material, the rest is easy for Black.

MOBILIZE POTENTIAL PASSED PAWNS

EUWE—EVANS

New York 1951

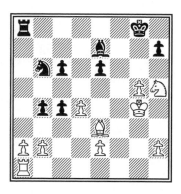

Diagram 32

Black moves. He has a semi-mobile Q-side pawn mass coupled with control of the open a-file. The problem is to force a passed pawn in such a manner that it will be decisive. Note that Black's extraordinary pawn mobility more than compensates for the pawn which he is behind. Here is a case where Pawn Structure outweighs a disadvantage in Force.

1...b3 2 d5. A desperate bid to free his pieces. Also inadequate is 2 a3 c3! 3 bxc3 Nc4 4 Bf4 b2 5 Rb1 Rxa3. **Nxd5 3 Bd4 bxa2 4 Nf6+ Bxf6 5 gxf6 Nb4 6 Kf4 Kf7.** Safer than 6...Nc2 7 Rg1+. Now there is no good defense against Nc2. **7 Be5 Nc2.** Black wins. This is a good example against a former world champion of converting Pawn Structure into Force.

CONNECTED, ISOLATED AND BACKWARD PAWNS

CONNECTED PAWNS

Connected pawns are a strong formation because they are in a position to provide mutual defense. They may be either mobile or immobile depending on the array of enemy units opposing them. Pawns on adjacent files which can defend each other, when advanced, are said to be connected.

Diagram 33

DISCONNECTED OR ISOLATED PAWNS

SPLIT PAWNS

Isolated pawns (sometimes called "isolanis") are generally weak because they provide a target and are susceptible to blockade. They often resemble split pins in bowling and must be defended with pieces, not other pawns, which is highly uneconomical. Isolated pawns may be passed or not, again depending on the placement of the opposing units. The distinguishing characteristic of an isolated pawn is that there is no pawn of the same color behind it on either adjacent file.

Diagram 34

ARTIFICIALLY ISOLATED PAWN

White's pawn on d6 is artificially isolated because there is no pawn next to it that can immediately spring to its defense. It differs from an isolated pawn in that it does have pawns on either or both adjacent files.

Diagram 35

BACKWARD PAWN

Black's pawn on d6 is backward. We generally think of a pawn as having become isolated after it has advanced too far beyond the ken of the other pawns. However, a pawn can become isolated when it has not advanced far enough. This is called a backward pawn. It meets all the requirements of an isolated pawn inasmuch as there is no pawn of the same color behind it on an adjacent file.

Diagram 36

BACKWARD PAWN ON OPEN FILE

Black's pawn on d6 is backward on an open file (typically arising from the Sicilian Defense). This is a glaring weakness because enemy forces now have access to it via the open d-file. The main difference is that a backward pawn is physically unable to advance while a backward pawn on an open file is free to do so, but only at the cost of its life.

Diagram 37

BLOCKADE ISOLATED PAWNS

BOULACHANIS—EVANS

Olympiad 1950

Diagram 38

White moves. An isolated pawn is weak mainly for two reasons: (1) it cannot be defended by another pawn behind it; (2) it cannot control the square directly in front of it and can be blockaded on this square. Once an isolani is anaesthetized, it throws other pieces on the defensive.

1 Qd3. Loses the d-pawn without a fight. Better is 1 Bc4 Rac8 2 Rxc8 Rxc8 3 Bxd5 Nxd5 4 Rc1 trying to hold a difficult ending. Incidentally 1 Nd7 would not do owing to Qg5 2 g3 Bxb3 winning a piece. **Bxb3 2 Qxb3 Rxd4 3 Re1 Rd2 4 f3 Nd5 5 Rc4 Bc5+ 6 Kh1 Bf2 6 Ree4 Rd8 8 Rc1 Ne3 9 Bd3 Qg5 10 g4 Qh4.** It's amazing how quickly White disintegrated once the d4 pawn fell. Notice the methodical invasion on the weak dark square complex.

TRY TO MOBILIZE ISOLATED PAWNS

EVANS—BISGUIER

New York 1955

Diagram 39

Black moves. We saw the consequences of a blockaded, isolated pawn in the previous example. An isolani is strong under two conditions: (1) if it exerts a cramping influence on the enemy; (2) if it can be liquidated at will. Here both of these conditions are fulfilled.

1...d4. He is in a big rush to dissolve the isolani fearing it might remain there forever after 1...Re8 2 b5 Ne7 3 Na4 Bxb2 4 Nxb2. **2 exd4 Nxd4 3 Nb5.** Seeking simplification because Black's pieces already are crawling all over the center. If 3 Bd3 Bg4 is hard to meet. **Nxe2+ 4 Qxe2 Bxb2 5 Qxb2 Qb6 Draw agreed.** The balanced Pawn Structure offers little hope of any progress. Since neither side expects the other to make a mistake, and since White has lost his theoretical opening advantage of the first move, there is not much reason to continue the battle.

TRY TO REPAIR ISOLATED PAWNS

EVANS—POSCHEL

U.S. Championship 1948

Diagram 40

White moves. The principle of repairing weaknesses holds true for Time and Space as well as Pawn Structure. For a long time White had been seeking a way to eliminate his laggard e-pawn. This gave rise to an alert combination based on the momentary pin of Black's d-pawn. What is it?

1 e5! Nxe5 Loses a piece but it's hard to suggest better. If 1...b5 2 exd6. Or 1...Rd8 2 Na5! Nxe5 3 Bxe5 Qxe5 4 Qxb7+ Kd7 5 Qc6+ Ke6 6 Qxa6 Qe1+ 7 Rf1 Qe3+ 8 Kh1. **2 Nxe5 Bxe5 3 Rxf8+ Qxf8 4 Bxe5 c5.** Black relied on this to regain the piece. **5 Qf4! 1-0.** Here is a case where, as often happens, tactics supplement strategy. White's long range strategy was to get rid of his isolated e-pawn. Tactics presented him with the proper moment to do so.

PILE UP ON TARGETS

EVANS—STEINER

1st match game 1952

Diagram 41

White moves. Black's isolated a-pawn is a target in the direct firing line of an open file. In the endgame this very pawn would be decisive—simply remove all the pieces from the board except the kings and ...a5 wins. Yet, as Tarrasch said, the gods have placed the middle game before the ending. And here White is ideally poised to exploit the target.

1 Ne5! Very logical, seeking to dislodge the knight on c6 which defends a7. If now 1...Nxe5 2 dxe5 Nd5 3 Bd4! wins the pawn on a7 while preserving the two bishops. **Ne4 2 Be1.** Of course 2 Qxa7 is playable, but there's no rush and Bxe6 is an additional threat. **Rfc8 4 Bd3.** Still no rush. A new threat is 5 Rxc6 Rxc6 6 Bxe4. **Nf6 5 Qxa7.** Finally the target falls. White is a pawn ahead and the rest was a matter of technique.

MAINTAIN ACCESS TO BACKWARD PAWNS

RESHEVSKY—D. BYRNE

New York 1955

Diagram 42

White moves. Black just captured a knight on d5 and White must decide whether to recapture with the pawn or queen—a difficult choice. If the backward pawn on d6 remains on a closed file, then it is hard to reach it. But when exposed on an open file it's easier to exert pressure on this target.

1 cxd5 Not an error but strategically wrong because it closes the d-file. After 1 Qxd5! the question becomes whether Black can enforce ...d5 to dissolve his backward pawn on d6. One possibility is 1...Ne7 2 Qd2 d5 3 Bxe7! Kxe7 4 Rad1 d4 (4... dxc4? 5 Qb4+ costs the queen) 5 exd4 exd4 6 Qb4+ winning. Passive defense also fails after 1 Qxd5 Bf8 2 Rad1 Be7 3 Rd2 0-0 4 Rfd1 piling up on the target. **1...Ne7 2 e4 f5 3 f3 g5 4 Qd3 0-0 5 Rac1.** White had no time to profit from control of the open c-file and the game soon ended in a draw after **5... fxe4 6 fxe4 h5 7 Rxf8+ Rxf8 8 Rf1 Rxf1 9 Kxf1 Kf7 10 Kg2 Kg6 11 h3 Ng8 12 Nc3 Nf6.**

TRY TO BLOCK ACCESS TO BACKWARD PAWNS

JACOBS—EVANS

U.S. Open Championship 1955

Diagram 43

Black moves. When defending a backward pawn on an open file, your strategy should be to force your opponent to close his access to it. Black has a glaring weakness on d6 but if he can cause White to play Nd5 so that, in the subsequent exchange, White will have to recapture with a pawn instead of his queen, then the d-file will be closed and Black's problem is solved.

1...Nb6! Threatening Nxc4 **2 Bb3 Bg4** A little finesse before returning to e6 which probably should be done right away. **3 Ne1** To prevent the doubled pawns after ...Bxf3 but much more active is 3 c5! **Rc8 4 Qd3 Be6 5 Bxf6 Bxf6 6 Nd5** Finally forced, the only way to defend c4. **Nxd5 7 exd5 Bd7.** Compare this position with the diagram. Black has achieved his primary goal by converting his pawn on d6 into a bastion of strength. White has been forced to close the d-file and in the process Black acquired the two bishops. Also Black threatens to expand later with f5. White must now fight for the draw and, in fact, succumbed in another dozen moves.

REPAIR BACKWARD PAWNS

FINKELSTEIN—EVANS

New York 1947

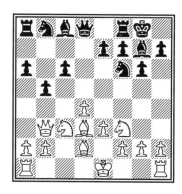

Diagram 44

Backward pawns provide natural targets and restrict freedom of movement. It stands to reason they should be repaired (or dissolved) by any available means—tactical or otherwise. In diagrams 44-46 Black utilizes the precious move to repair his Pawn Structure.

Black moves. **1...c5!** Exploits the pin on the d3 bishop to and gets rid of the backward c-pawn. It gains a tempo because White must delay castling owing to the threat of c4 and also unseals the lovely h1-a8 diagonal after his bishop goes to b7. Note that the tempting developing move 1...Be6? does not solve the problem of the backward c-pawn after White retreats 2 Qc2. Then 2...c5 could be met by the simple 3 dxc5.

ROSS—EVANS

New York 1949

Diagram 45

Black moves. This time Black exploits the indirect pin of White's e-pawn with 1...d5! because 2 Nxd5? Nxd5 3 Qxd5 Qxd5 4 exd5 Bxf5 wins a piece. Now on 2 Ng3 d4 3 Nb1 Nc6 Black seizes the initiative.

GOLDWATER—EVANS

New York 1949

Diagram 46

Black moves. He advances this backward pawn without further ado with **1...e5!** There isn't as much need for haste as in the last two diagrams because Black even can take time to develop with 1...Bd6 first. However e5 must be played eventually and there is no reason to wait. The game continued **2 dxe5 Ndxe5 3 Bc2 Bg4 4 h3 Bxf3 5 Nxf3 Nxf3+ 6 Qxf3 Qxf3 7 gxf3.** White has a horrible Pawn Structure and lost the endgame.

The moral: When pawns are mobile they are healthy.

DOUBLED AND TRIPLED PAWNS

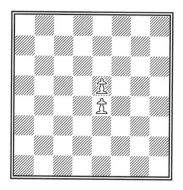

Diagram 47

DOUBLED PAWNS

Doubled pawns usually should be avoided because they are so hard to mobilize. However, they frequently offer Space compensation, inasmuch as they provide an open file on which to operate.

Diagram 48

TRIPLED PAWNS

Tripled pawns represent the worst possible formation, with the possible exception of quadrupled pawns. They can be capped by only one enemy pawn to hold them at bay, as shown here,

IMMOBILE DOUBLED PAWNS

ADAMS—EVANS_____

U.S. Championship 1948

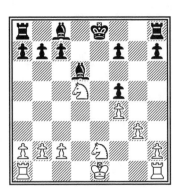

Diagram 49

White moves. When doubled pawns are there to stay—beware! All too often one of them can be picked off if your opponent focuses on them with a laser.. Here White merely maneuvers his knights to d4 and e3 and even the two bishops are of no avail. Note how Black would stand well if only his pawn were on g7 instead of f5. **1 Nd4 c6.** Equally futile is 1...c5 2 Nb5 Kd7 3 0-0-0. **2 Ne3 0-0 3 0-0-0.** Adding insult to injury! The pawn can't run away—White can capture it at his leisure—so he strengthens his position first by castling. **Bc5 4 Nexf5.** White has won a pawn and the rest is a matter of technique, a phrase you will see many times in this book.

DOUBLE-EDGED DOUBLED PAWNS

HOROWITZ—EVANS

New York 1951

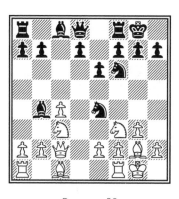

Diagram 50

Black moves. He has a genuine dilemma: Whether to double the pawns by Nxc3 or Bxc3. Each move has its peculiar drawbacks and advantages. Which would you choose and why?

1...Nxc3. Loses a vital tempo and gives White a Time-Space edge which offsets his bad Pawn Structure. How this conflict is resolved in the game is instructive. Back then I was overly fond of preserving the two bishops. Today I'd play 1... Bxc3 2 bxc3 Qa5 3 Bb2 b6 4 Nd2 Nxd2 5 Qxd2 Rb8. **2 bxc3 Be7 3 Nd4 d6.** Playable but inconsistent is 3...d5 4 cxd5 exd5 which would undo all Black's labor by letting White dissolve his doubled pawns. **4 Rd1 Qc7.** More prudent was 4...a6. Now Black must undergo contortions. **5 Nb5 Qb8.** Fighting to make sure the doubled pawns stay doubled. White keeps an edge after 5...Qxc4 6 Nxd6 Qa6 7 Qd3. **6 Ba3 Rd8 7 Qd3.** An alternative is 4 c5 dxc5 (not 1...d5? 2 c6! Bxa3 3 c7! snuffs the queen) 5 Rxd8+ Bxd8 6 Bxc5 Bd7. **Ne8 8 c5 d5 9 c4 a6 10 Nc3.** Better is 10 Nd6! Nxd6 11 cxd6 Bxd6 12 cxd5 Be5 13 Rac1 exd5 14 Bxd5 Be6 15 e4. **d4 11 Na4 Qc7 12 Rab1 Rb8.** Finally Black is no longer cramped and out of danger. In retrospect 1...Bxc3 was an easier defense.

CAPTURE TOWARDS THE CENTER

EVANS—J. CROSS

U.S. Open Championship 1953

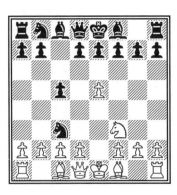

Diagram 51

White moves. Sometimes doubled pawns are inevitable, as in this variation of the Sicilian Defense: **1 e4 c5 2 Nf3 Nf6**

3 e5 Nd5 4 Nc3 Nxc3. The problem is whether White should recapture with the d or b pawn. Right now Time is more important than Pawn Structure, so **5 dxc3!** capturing *away* from the center is the exception that proves the rule. It frees the bishop on c1 and retains the initiative. If 1...d5 6 exd6 Qxd6 7 Qxd6 exd6 8 Bf4 is clearly in White's favor. On 1...Nc6 2 Bf4 reinforces the pawn on e5 and keeps Black cramped.

5 bxc3. Despite the temptation to choose the line which offers more rapid development, I followed the old rule of capturing **towards** the center because in the long run I feared an endgame where Black's 3 queenside pawns might hold White's 4 queenside pawns at bay. The reasoning here is similar to diagram 16, only in this case White does not obtain the two bishops to compensate for an inferior Pawn Structure. **5...d5 6 exd6 Qxd6 7 d4 cxd4?** Black should be reluctant to swap and keep the c-pawns doubled. He has nothing to fear from 7... e6 8 Ba3 Nd7. **8 cxd4.** Undoubling the pawns. The chances are now roughly equal.

IMMOBILE TRIPLED PAWNS

SMYSLOV—EVANS

Diagram 52

Black moves. The reason tripled pawns are bad, especially in the endgame, is they they cannot be mobilized. This is a drastic case. Black is a pawn up, but it matters not. In effect the tripled pawns count as one, so Black is in reality a pawn down! **1...f4.** Forced. If White had a pawn on f4, it would be stalemate. **2 gxf4 f5 3 Kc6 f6.** Again forced. Not 3...Ka7 4 Kc7. **4 Kd6!** Black was hoping in vain for stalemate after 4 Kb6. **Kxb7 5 Ke6. 1-0.** White eats the pawns at his leisure. A likely continuation might be 5...Kc7 6 Kxf5 Kd7 7 Kxf6.

TRANSITION TO ENDGAME

SMYSLOV—BOTVINNIK

7th match game 1954

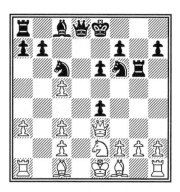

Diagram 53

Black moves. White is a pawn ahead; albeit tripled, it exerts considerable pressure and the immediate threat is Ng3. Black finds a witty way to swap queens which leaves his king in a strongly centralized post for the endgame. Just as each reduction in Force favors the side with superior Force, it also favors the side with the superior Pawn Structure, which looms more valuable as the endgame approaches because it is durable rather than transient in nature (like Time).

1...Ng4 2 Qxe4. Willingly entering the endgame despite the triplets. A good alternative is 2 Qd2 Qh4 3 g3 Qe7 4 Qd6. **Qd1+! 3 Kxd1 Nxf2+ 4 Ke1 Nxe4.** Black's strategy has borne fruit, though White is still on top thanks to his two bishops. The ending ran an interesting course which White, in fact, eventually won after **5 Nf4 Rg8 6 Bd3 Nxc5 7 Bxh7 Rh8 8 Bd3 Nxd3+ 9 cxd3 Bd7 10 Be3 0-0-0 11 Kf2** with a dangerous passed h-pawn.

WEAK SQUARES

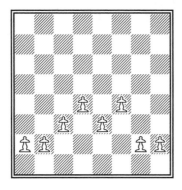

Diagram 54

A LIGHT SQUARE WEAKNESS

A weak square complex is a series of similar colored squares which can never again be defended by pawns because the pawns (or pawn) behind them have already advanced. Remember—pawns cannot retreat! That's the reason why unnecessary or prolific pawn moves early in the game are ill-advised. Incidentally, a weak square complex is even weaker when the bishop that would normally nurse it has been lost or swapped.

A hole is a square which can never again be defended by a pawn. In diagram 54 both d3 and e4 are holes for White.

Weak squares are characterized by a sense of emptiness. *When pawns are arrayed on black, the light squares are weak; when they are arrayed on white, the dark squares are weak.*

Whenever a pawn advances, a fresh weakness is incurred. Of course this doesn't mean that we should sun pawn moves altogether. But it means that they should be made sparingly, either to free the pieces or with some other positive objective in mind. Lasting sins are revealed in our Pawn Structure!

Diagram 55

WEAK "LUFT" VS. STRONG "LUFT"

Luft is the German word for air. If you are unfamiliar with "luft" or the need for it, consult diagram 120. In making an escape hatch for the king so that it doesn't get mated on the back rank, we are generally confronted with the choice of pushing either the h-pawn or the g-pawn. The h-pawn is usually advisable because it does not create any holes. In diagram 55 Black's formation involves two holes at a6 and c6. White created no holes because the slight weakening of g3 is offset by the presence of the f-pawn. Therefore White's configuration is more desirable.

AVOID NEEDLESS WEAKNESSES

EVANS—KRAUSS

Offhand game, New York 1945

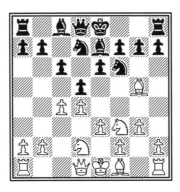

Diagram 56

Black moves. This message can never be repeated too often. When a beginner does not know what to do, he generally pushes the nearest piece of wood. Since the pawns are so numerous, this unlucky selection all too often falls on them. White just played g3. Why is this inferior, and what move would have been better?

The correct move was 1 Bd3 developing a piece and preparing to castle. Instead White has irreparably weakened the light squares on f3 and h3 by preparing to fianchetto his bishop on g2 where, in the words of Nimzovich, it would "bite on granite." The granite here refers to Black's solid pawn mass at d5, e6, c6. A fianchetto is recommended in closed positions only if there is a good chance that lines will be opened for the bishop in the ensuing action. Pieces usually should be developed in active, not passive posts.

OCCUPY HOLES

EVANS—JOYNER

U.S. Junior Championship 1948

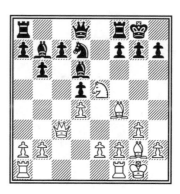

Diagram 57

White moves. Black has a gaping hole on c6. If it were his move, he could repair it with Bxe5 followed by c5 or c6. On principle White ought to occupy this hole with 1 Nc6—and he did.

1 Nc6! Qf6. If 1...Bxc6 2 Bxd6 cxd6 3 Qxc6 gains at least a pawn without allowing Black any counterplay. Another try is 1...Qe8 2 e3! Nf6 3 Rac1 with a bind. **2 Bxd6 Qxd6 3 Bxd5!** **Rfe8.** Not 3...Qxd5? 4 Ne7+ and Nxd5. **4 Bf3.** White has won a pawn and the rest is technique. If now 4...Bxc6 5 Bxc6 Rad8 6 e4 (or e3) is crushing.

EXPLOIT HOLES

FRANK—EVANS

U.S. Open Championship 1948

Diagram 58

Black moves. White has two gaping holes at h4 and f4. Black already occupies one with the rook and his task is to occupy the other. So ask yourself what piece Black wants there, and then how to get it there.

1...Nf8! The idea is to swing to g6 and then f4. **2 Ra1 Ng6 3 Bc1.** The hapless bishop can't guard everything at once. Now White invades on the hole just created on c3. **Rc3 4 Rd3 Qc7 5 Bxg5 Rxc2 6 Qe3 Rh8 7 Rc1?** Loses material. It's still a fight after 7 Re1 Kd7. **Rxc1 8 Qxc1 Qxc1 9 Bxc1 Nxe5.** Pawn Structure has finally been converted to Force. Black is a pawn up with an easy victory ahead. Notice, as so often happens, it is the *theme* or the *threat* of a given plan that leads to the win even though it may never be carried out. The need to stop the knight from reaching f4 induced White to leave his other hole on c3 unguarded.

PENETRATE WEAK SQUARES

EVANS—KESTEN

Olympics 1950

Diagram 59

White moves. By all standards d6 is a weak square because there is no pawn that can guard it. So White utilizes the pin on the e-pawn to transport his knight from a passive post on g3 to an active one on d6. This is a good example of converting Time into Space made possible by an opponent's weak square complex.

1 Nf5! Qc7 2 e5!? In a hurry to get to d6. The weakness of a square often must be evaluated in terms of what attacking pieces can penetrate it. This advance concedes Black d5 for his knight, but in chess as in advertising it pays to give a little in order to get a lot. Every advance creates a new weakness and this is no time to be niggardly! Black's knight can always be dislodged by the simple expedient of Bxd5 (after it gets there) whereas White's knight on d6 stands like a house. More patient, however, is 2 Rfe1 Kh8 3 Ne3. **fxe5 3 dxe5 Nd5?** Premature. Instead Black could sit pretty after 3...b5! 4.Ba2 c5. **4 Nd6.** The culmination of a spatial combination. White has the initiative and Black is cramped. Note that if Black had a sound Pawn Structure with a pawn on f7 instead of f6 there would have been no way to exploit the hole on d6.

The remaining moves were: **4...Re7 5 Nd4 a6 6 Bb3 c5 7 Nxe6 Nxe6 8 Nxb7 Ndf4 9 Nd6 Kh8 10 g3 Ng6 11 Qe4 Rf8 12 f4 Nd4 13 Bd5 Qd7 14 Rde1 Nb5 15 Nf7+ Rfxf7 16 Bxf7 Qd4+ 17 Qxd4 Nxd4 18 e6 Rc7 19 Bxg6 1-0.** On 19... hxg6 20 e7 the pawn sprints to glory.

INVADE WEAK SQUARES

EVANS—BISGUIER

New York State Championship 1949

Diagram 60

White moves. Material is even but Black's has an overwhelming control of the central files. His king is active, his pieces are centralized and there are weak squares on d3 and e3. Note the characteristic emptiness around these squares. Black's problem, which is solved instructively in the game, is how to invade on the e-file.

1 Bxe3. The king and pawn ending would be drawn **if** White could only get to it. Exchanges help—but he can't exchange all the pieces. **Nxe3 2 Rfe1 Nc2 3 Rxe8 Rxe8 4 Rd1 Re2.** This invasion is decisive. If now 5 Nc1 Rxg2! 6 Kxg2 (or 6 Rd7+ Ke8 7 Rxc7 Ne3) Ne3+ followed by Nxd1 wins. **5 g3 Ne3 6 Rb1 Nc4 7 Nd4 Rxb2 8 Rxb2 Nxb2 9 Nxf5 Nd1 10 c4 Kf6 11 Nd4 Ke5.** This king is just too active. **12 Nb3 b6 13 Kg1 c5 14 Kf1 Ne3+ 15 Ke2 Nxc4** and further resistance proved futile.

A RUDE SHOCK

KAUFMAN—EVANS_____

U.S. Open Championship 1955

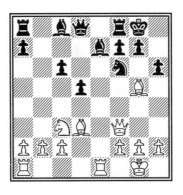

Diagram 61

White moves. This is a good example of why pawns should be pushed with extreme caution. Black just played h6? "putting the question to the bishop." The reply came as a rude shock. **1 Bxh6! gxh6 2 Qe3 Kg7** Returning the piece without a fight but it's hard to find a decent defense. If 2...Be6 3 Qxh6 Bd6 3 Qg5+ Kh8 4 Re3 d4 5 Rf3 is the quietus. Also inadequate is 2...d4 2 Qxh6 dxc3 3 Re5 threatening Rg5+. The game continued **3 Qxe7 Qxe7 4 Rxe7** snaring a pawn, though Black miraculously succeeded in drawing.

PAWN CHAINS

Diagram 62

A *healthy pawn chain* has its base either on or as near to its original square as possible. Here the pawn at e5 has its base on b2. Pawn chains, to be undermined, must be weakened at their base. Hence it stands to reason that the further this base is removed from enemy forces the harder it is to get at.

SICKLY PAWN CHAIN

Diagram 63

Note that the pawn is on b3 rather than b2. This pawn chain is slightly compromised because the pawn on e5 has only two links (d4 and c3) compared to three links in diagram 62.

A chain is thus a series of connected pawns which have reached a point at which the one furthest advanced is organically linked to the one which is least advanced. Pawn chains usually are as strong as their weakest link. Even when a pawn chain is healthy, it involves a weak square complex. In both of these diagrams White has light square weakness on d3, e4 and d5.

DISEASED PAWN CHAINS

MENGARINI—EVANS_____

U.S. Championship 1951

Diagram 64

White moves. Diseased pawns are characterized by overextended bases and lack of mobility. Here even opposite colored bishops don't help White because his pawns are so far advanced that they are ripe for the picking. Contrast them with Black's healthy kingside pawns with a sound base on f7.

1 Ke1. On 1 Be3 Be4 White is in "zugzwang" which means the unpleasant obligation to move. The bishop must then abandon the defense of f4. **Kxf4 2 Bd4 Ke4 3 Bc3 Ke3**

Kd1 Bg4+ 5 Kc1 Ke4 6 Kd2 Be2 7 Kc1 Bg4. Toying with White. There is no rush to go after the h-pawn. **8 Kd2 Be6 9 Kc1 Bb3 10 Kd2 Bc2 11 Kc1 Kf4 12 Bd4 Kg3 0-1.**

ADVANCED PAWN BASES

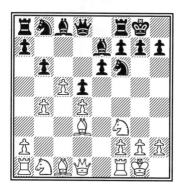

Diagram 65

Black moves. We already determined that a pawn chain is strongest when its base stands on the original second rank. The chain is weakened each time this base is advanced, so it's a good idea to lure it forward. Black has just played ...b6 provoking the reply b4 to support the pawn on c5. Now with one deft stroke Black cripples the advanced pawns.

1...a5! 2 Bd2. What else? There is no satisfactory reply. If 2 a3 axb4 snags a pawn because of the pin on the a-file. Note that if Black did not play 1...a5 immediately, then White would have had time for Bb2 to defend the rook on a1 and play a3. **axb4 3 Bxb4 Na6 4.Bxa6 Bxa6 5 Re1 bxc5 6 Bxc5 Bxc5 7 dxc5 Qc7 8 Qc2 Rfc8.** White's Pawn Structure is shattered and he is saddled with a c5 pawn under constant fire. If 9 Rc1 Ne4 10 c6 Bc4 does the trick.

STRIKE CHAINS AT THEIR BASE

ADAMS—EVANS

New York 1951

Diagram 66

Black moves. He must find a way to strike at the pawn on f4 to undermine the pawn on e5. Striking at the base is as simple as pricking a balloon with a pin—everything explodes. .

1...g5! Literally smashing the kingside to destroy the pawn chain at f4 and e5. Is it worth it? In the endgame, of course, such a move would be played only after the most extreme deliberation. But this is not the endgame, it is still the middle game. Black reckons that his influence in the center is more important *right now* than Pawn Structure. **2 f5.** 2 fxg5 Nxe5 gives Black a beautifully centralized game while White's pieces are awkwardly cluttered. Incidentally 2 0-0-0 is out of the question because of 3...gxf4 4 Bxf4 e3 followed by Bxh1 winning the Exchange. **Qxe5 3 fxe6 fxe6 4 h4 Bc5 5 0-0-0 Nb6 6 hxg5 Nd5 7 Rh6 0-0 8 Rxe6.** Relatively better is 8 Kb1. **Qxe6 0-1.** After 9 Nxe6 Bxe3+ 10 Kb1 Rxf2 the queen is no match for the minor pieces. Notice how quickly White fell apart once his center collapsed.

UNDERMINE STRONG BASES

EVANS—DAKE

U.S. Open Championship 1955

Diagram 67

White moves. Black's setup looks sound. Upon closer examination, however, we see that the dark squares on his kingside (h6 and f6) are weak holes and most of his pieces are clustered on the queenside. Thus it seems like a propitious moment to storm his fortress. In order to do this White must somehow invade at g6. Before this can be done the base pawn at f7 must be undermined.

1 f5! The idea is to strike at the base with e6. **Nbd7.** Attempting to bring a knight which is out-of-play to the aid of his embattled monarch. Black is already crumbling. If 1...Rd8 2 Rxd8+ Bxd8 3 e6! fxe6 4 fxg6 leaves his Pawn Structure in shambles. **2 e6 Nf8 3 exf7+ Kxf7 4 Ne5+ Kg7 5 Ng4 Ncd7 6 Bd4+ Kf7 7 Re1.** It's incredible how quickly Black fell apart. There is now no good defense against Nh6+ followed by f6. Note that in the original diagram even were Black's pawn on g7 White would still have a strong attack with f5, but it would be harder to make headway.

EXPOSE ENEMY BASES

EVANS—ADAMS

New Jersey 1950

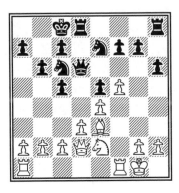

Diagram 68

White moves. His pawn chain extends from c2 to f5. Were it Black's move 1...c4 would undermine the chain by shifting the base from c2 to d3 after the consequent exchange of pawns. If White takes time to stop c4, then Black can play f6 consolidating his own chain from g7 to e5.

1 f6! Using this pawn as a battering ram in order to double Black's pawns on the open f-file. The sacrifice is only temporary, and the clearing of the g-file is not dangerous because Black can't make use of it to attack. This game is instructive because it emphasizes the long-term importance of destroying a pawn chain even at the short-term cost of a pawn. **gxf6 2 Ng3!** White must continue sharply, spurning 2 Bxh6? f5! **c4!** The principle is that an attack on the wing is best met by a reaction in the center. **3 Rad1 cxd3 4 cxd3 Nd4 5 Qf2 f5 6 Bxd4 Qxd4 7 Qxd4 Rxd4 8 Nxf5 Nxf5 9 Rxf5.** Note that both sides now have exposed bases: White on d3 and Black on f7. Now speed is of the essence in the race to queen a pawn. **Rhd8 10 Rxf7 Rxd3 11 Rxd3 Rxd3 12 Rf6 Rd2.** Not 12...Rd6? 13 Rxd6 cxd6 14 Kf2 Kd7 15 Kf3 Ke6 16 g4 d5 17 exd5+ Kxd5 18 h4 and White wins by virtue of that old weevil, the outside passed pawn. **13 Rxh6 Rxb2 14 g4 Re2 15 h4 c5 16 h5 Kd7 17 Rh7+ Kd6 18 h6 c4 19 Rh8 Rxe4 20 h7 Rxg4+ 21 Kf2 Rh4 22 Rd8+ Kc5 23.h8/Q Rxh8 24 Rxh8 Kd4 25 Ke2 Kc3 26 Ra8 b5 27 Rxa7 b4 28 Rc7 1-0.** Black missed some better moves in the ending, but White followed a consistent theme by converting Time into superior Pawn Structure at the cost of Force (1 f6!). His better Pawn Structure was later converted into Force when Black had to sacrifice his rook to prevent the h-pawn from queening. A game of chess is an organic whole.

THE BAD BISHOP

WHITE HAS THE BAD BISHOP— BLACK HAS THE GOOD BISHOP

There is no theology in chess. When a bishop is bad it is not wicked, just ineffective. Diagram 69 is drawn because neither side can penetrate but it's apparent that a good bishop commands mobility and open lines, whereas a bad bishop is hemmed in by its own pawns. Generally it's a good idea to place pawns on a color opposite that of the bishop. When this is impossible, try to swap the bishop. Note that White has no piece that can attack the pawn on b5, whereas his own bishop is tied down to the defense b4.

Pawn Structure intimately affects the working value of the pieces. Bishops are more effective on an open board. Conversely, with two knights vs. two bishops, try to close the position because knights have the power to leap over obstacles, barricades, and tall buildings.

Diagram 69

WHITE HAS A GOOD KNIGHT— BLACK HAS A BAD BISHOP

Black moves. Here is a drastic example of paralysis, known in chess jargon as a "bind." White has a stranglehold on the dark squares and his knight irradiates sunshine compared to the dour bishop on c8 that lacks scope. Black has no counterplay and is helpless against Ra3 followed by Rxa5 and the eventual advance of his a-pawn. Rather than wait for the hearse to arrive, Black resigned on the spot.

HALPER—EVANS

Diagram 70

GOOD KNIGHT VS. BAD BISHOP

GOMPERT—EVANS

New York 1946

Diagram 71

White moves. In the Marshall Club Junior Championship, my first tournament, I learned the power of a centralized knight. White's pawns are all on the same color as his hapless bishop, and there is no way to prevent Black's invasion on the light squares. The threat is ...Rh2 followed by Ree2. **1 Rd3.** Desperately trying to bring this rook into play at the cost of a pawn. White can hold out longer but still is lost after 1 Rd1 Rh2 2 Rd2 Rh1. **Rxb2 2 Rd2 Rb3+ 3 Kg2 Rxa3.** Black's two extra pawns assure an easy win.

THE QUEENSIDE MAJORITY

Diagram 72

Black has a potential outside passed pawn. The queenside majority, characterized by an unbalanced pawn structure, generally leads to sharp play because the themes are so forcibly outlined. To draw this ending White must play e4 and maintain the pawn on this square to confine the enemy king . Thus 1 e4 Kf8 2 Kf1 f5 3 f3! equalizes.

EXPLOIT THE QUEENSIDE MAJORITY

EVANS—POMAR

U.S. Open Championship 1954

Diagram 73

White moves. His task is how to cash in on his queenside majority (2 pawns vs. 1) by demolishing the blockade and mobilizing the potential passed pawn. This is easily remedied by tactical means.

1 b6! This temporary pawn sacrifice gets the a-pawn moving. **axb6.** Forced. If 1...c4 2 b7 Rb8 3 Rxc4 followed by Rc8. The game concluded: **2 a7 Ra8 3 Rb2 c4 4 Rxb6 c3 5 Rb7+ Kd6 6 Ra6+ Kc5 7 Ke3 c2 8 Kd2 f5 9 gxf5 exf5 10 Rb8 1-0.** White wins a rook. Notice how easily his king stops the c-pawn whereas Black's king can't cross scene of action.

MOBILIZE THE QUEENSIDE MAJORITY

EVANS—KALME

Hollywood 1954

Diagram 74

White moves. For the nonce White is apparently stymied on the queenside because 1 b5 seems to lose a pawn. Not so— tactics provide the answer. Notice how in the sequence Black's proud pawn on d5 becomes transformed into a scraggly isolani.

1 b5! The blockade on c6 must be demolished! **cxb5.** No better is 1...Bxd4 2 Qxd4 cxb5 3 Bh6 f6 4 Bxf8 Rxf8 5 c6. The game concluded: **2 c6 Qd8 3 axb5 Bxd4 4 Qxd4 Nxb5 5 Qb2 Nc7 6 Bh6 f6 7 Bxf8 Qxf8 8 Re1 Kf7 9 Qb7 Qd6 10 Rxe6! Qxe6 11 Bxd5! Qxd5 12 Qxc8 Ne6 13 Qxc8 Ne6 14 c7 Ng5 14 Qe8+ 1-0.** If 14...Kxe8 15 c8/Q+ Qd8 16 Re1+ Kf7 17 Qxd8 wins.

THE MINORITY ATTACK

EVANS—OPSAHL

Olympics 1950

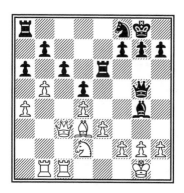

Diagram 75

Black moves. We already examined the power of mobilizing the queenside majority. Here White has taken active measures to neutralize Black's majority by launching "the minority attack." The net aim of using his two pawns on that wins as battering rams is to convert Black's potential strength into a weakness instead. Meanwhile care must be taken to meet Black's budding kingside offensive.

1...axb5 2 axb5 Bh3 3 g3 Rae8 4 bxc6 bxc6 5 Bf1! In annotating this in his book *The Most Instructive Games of Chess Ever Played,* Irving Chernev wrote:

> *"Excellent! White sees to it that his king is properly protected before starting an attack on the weak pawn. White has accomplished what he set out to do with the Minority Attack. He has saddled Black with a backward pawn on an open file—a pawn which is vulnerable to attack as it dare not advance, and can be defended only with pieces. Against this weakling White will direct his*

fire. Had White been hasty and played 5 Rb6 instead, the consequences would have been painful: 5...Rxe3! 6 fxe3 Qxe3+ 7 Kh1 Qf2 (threatens mate on the move) 8 Rg1 Re1! and White is faced with four threats of mate on the move!"

Diagram 76

19 MOVES LATER...

White moves. This position was reached after many pieces were exchanged. Black must nurse his neurotic c-pawn.. **1 Nc5+ Kf6 2 Nd7+ Ke6 3 Nf8+ Kf6.** Always forced. Not 3... Kd6 4 Rd7 mate. **4 Nh7+ Ke6 5 Ng5+ Kd6** The last chance avoid losing a pawn was 5...Kf6 6 f3! Ra2+ 7 Ke1! and now if 7...Rxh2 8 e4 threatens e5+. **6 Rb7 f6 7 Nh7 Ke6 8 Nf8+ Kf7 9 Nxg6 Kxg6 10 Rxe7** White snared a pawn by a curious knight's tour, converting Pawn Structure into Force, but the win is still hard. **Kf5 11 Rc7 Rc1 12 Rc8 Kg6 13 Kg3 Rc2 14 h4 Kf5 15 Rh8 Kg6 16 f5+ Kxf5.** A tougher defense is 16...Kg7 17 Rc8 (the rook can't get out after 17 Rxh5) Rc1 18 Rc7+ Kg8 19 f3 Rc4) **17 Rxh5+ Kg6 18 Rh8 Kf5 19 Rg8 Rc1 20 Kg2 Ra1 21 h5 Ra7 22 Rg3 Rh7 23 Rh3 Kg5 24 Kf3 Rh6 25 Rh1 Kf5 26 Kg3 Kg5 27 Rh4 Kf5 28 Rf4+ Kg5 29 Rg4+ Kf5.** The key point is 29...Kxh5 30 Rh4+ Kg5

31 Rxh6 Kxh6 32 Kg4 Kg6 33 Kf4 wins. This happens later.
30 Kh4 Rh8 31 Rg7 Ra8 32 h6 Ra1 33 Rg3 Rh1+ 34 Rh3 Rg1 35 Rf3+! Careless is 35 h5? Rg4+ 36 Kh5 Rg5+ drawing by perpetual check. **Kg6 36 Rg3+ Rxg3 37 Kxg3 Kxh6 38 Kg4 Kg6 39 Kf4 Kg7 40 Kf5 Kf7 41 f3 1-0.**

The actual game lasted 81 moves, the last and longest one in Chernev's book, which he dubbed *A Symphony of Heavenly Length:*

> *"To call this game a masterpiece is to do it insufficient justice. It is more than that. It is a symphony played over a chessboard with an orchestra of pieces and pawns…You may get the idea from the foregoing that I am wild about this game, and that I wish it lasted more than the 81 moves it does. If you do, then I have conveyed the right idea."*

FORCE

Force is the fist of the chessboard. And in a purely physical struggle, the stronger is bound to win. So it is with chess. "When right opposes right, force decides"—or might makes right!

Material superiority is decisive when all other things are equal. (Of course there are exceptions, such as two knights can't compel mate against a lone king.) In practice "other things" are seldom "equal." It seems like there are always little obstacles to be surmounted. One side can be a pawn ahead in a simple endgame yet still draw because of stalemate or opposite colored bishops. In a gambit one side can be two rooks ahead yet still get mated because of a deficit in Time and/or Space (see diagram 1 (p. 14)). Our task is to weigh an advantage in one element against a disadvantage in another element, which is essentially a problem in evaluation (see chapter 7).

Checkmate is our goal, and the accumulation of superior Force is the chief means to that end. Of all the elements Force is the most important and in itself comes closest to being the most decisive. Generally an advantage in another element culminates in or must first be converted into Force before it becomes decisive. Reuben Fine expressed this with the quip, "I'd rather have a pawn than a finger!" A test of one's technical skill is how easily one can convert Force into victory.

TABLE OF RELATIVE VALUES

The following table is based on centuries of experience and weighs the abstract value of the pieces in relation to each other. One unit is the smallest measure of strength.

Pawn	=	1 unit
Knight	=	3½ units
Bishop	=	3½ units
Rook	=	5 units
Queen	=	10 units

Another way of expressing it is in terms of money. A pawn is worth 10¢, knights and bishops 35¢ apiece, the rook 50¢, and the queen a dollar. The king has no fixed value. In the opening where it must seek shelter and take no active role in the action, it's worth about 20¢. In the endgame, however, where it may wander freely without fear of getting mated, it becomes a valuable attacking unit worth about 40¢.

The important thing to remember is that this table expresses abstract relationships under ideal conditions. Values change as positions change. Sometimes a well-placed minor piece (bishop or knight) is worth more than a rook,. A pawn that can't be stopped from queening is obviously worth more than the same pawn under ordinary conditions.

Superior force confers about the same edge as starting a poker game with more chips. You can crowd a foe with bigger bets until he is bankrupt.

SUPERIOR FORCE WINS

Diagram 77

White wins whoever moves. The smallest unit of Force is the pawn, and here the win is elementary. White must only be careful not to permit Black's king to get in front of the pawn. Thus if **1...Kd5 2 Kf5!** But not 2 e4+? Ke6=. **Kd6 3 e4 Ke7 4 Ke5! Kd7.** This king cannot stay in front of the pawn because White has the opposition. Black has free will to the extent that he can choose his method of death. **5 Kf6 Ke8 6 Ke6! Kd8 7 Kf7 Kd7 8 e5** and the pawn is chaperoned to the queening square on e8. White on move is even simpler because **1 e4** would win immediately.

PATTERN FOR CONVERTING FORCE INTO VICTORY

Once having won material, if there is no quick win in sight, the general pattern is to steer for the endgame by swapping pieces. We have seen that even the lowly pawn acquires Herculean properties in the ending.

Diagram 78

White wins easily by swapping pieces: **1 Rxe7 Rxe7 2 Rxe7 Kxe7 3 Ke2** and then advancing the a-pawn and using his king to munch on Black's vulnerable kingside pawns. Conversely if it were Black's move, his best chance to draw consists in preserving one rook by **1...Rxe2 2 Rxe2 Ra8.**

THE TWO BISHOPS

In theory a knight is equal to a bishop; they each tally 3½ units in the table of relative values. Yet in practice a bishop often is preferable to a knight, especially in open positions and the endgame where it can sweep the board. Two bishops against two knights confer an advantage in Space rather than Force. Woe unto him who swaps bishop for knight without just cause!

The knight's range is more limited than the bishop, which helps explain why two bishops working in unison gain in strength as the endgame approaches. If you find yourself with bishop and knight against two bishops, try to swap one of the bishops. An exception is when the Pawn Structure is so locked that bishops are a liability because their range is seriously impaired. Since it is easier to open a game at will than to close it, the player with two bishops usually profits from the consequent opening of lines.

PLAY FOR THE BISHOP PAIR

EVANS—FINE

New York 1951

Diagram 79

Black moves. The two bishops usually constitute a powerful weapon. But they are not inherited, an active effort must be made to "win" them in the middle game. If a knight is also worth 3½ units, one may well be justified in demanding to know why such a fuss is being made about the bishop pair. The reason is that a century of chess theory has taught us a bishop in most positions is probably worth about 3¾ units.

1...Nf4! Hoping for 2 Qxd8? Nxe2+ 3 Kh1 Rxd8 which regains the pawn and also "wins" the two bishops in the process. I must confess that this move came as something of a shock to me. **2 Qc2 Nxg2 3 Nxg2 Qa5 4 Bd2.** White should not try to hold onto the pawn by 4 Be3 Bf5 5 Qc1 Rac8 regaining the pawn with advantage. **Qxc5 5 Qxc5 Nxc5 6 Bc3 e5.** To preserve two bishops. **7 Bb4 b6 8 Nc3** and the game was eventually drawn.

TWO BISHOPS VS. TWO KNIGHTS

BISGUIER—KASHDAN

Hollywood 1954

Diagram 80

White moves. Two bishops working in unison sweep the board when lines are open. This looks like an easy draw because material is even, but the winning process consists of (1) hemming in the knights with pawns; (2) tying them down to the defense of a weakness; (3) making inroads with the king; (4) liquidating pieces at a favorable moment. This ideal formula arises more frequently than one might imagine.

1 b4 axb4 2 axb4 Ne6. On 2...Na6 3 Bc3 followed by Kd4 also squeezes Black to death. **3 Ba4.** Threatening Bxd7. Notice that the knight on d7 is tied down to the defense of the weak b-pawn. **Nef8.** The exchange does not help. E.g., 3...Nxd4 4 Kxd4 Nf6 5 c5 bxc5 6 Kxc5 and the outside passed pawn is decisive. **4 Ke4 Kd6 5 Bxd7 Nxd7 6 Bxb6! f5+.** Equally hopeless is 6...Nxb6 7 c5+ Kc6 8 cxb6 Kxb6 9 Ke5 and Black's kingside pawns are easy prey. **7 Bd4.** White won by converting his Space advantage into Force.

TWO BISHOPS VS. BISHOP AND KNIGHT

BURGER—EVANS

U.S. Open Championship 1952

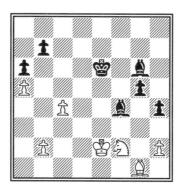

Diagram 81

Black moves. Two bishops are a powerful team because by virtue of their sweep and range they are capable of controlling both light and dark squares at the same time. White's weak queenside pawns have advanced to the point where they have trouble protecting each other, his bishop is lifeless and his knight is limited in scope. Black's bishop on f4 ties White to the defense of h2 while his comrade harasses the other wing.

1...Be5 2 b3 Bc2 3 Nd3. Of no avail is 3 b4 Bc3. **Bxd3+ 4 Kxd3 g4 5 Ke4 h3 6 b4 g3 7 hxg3 Bxg3 0-1.** White must lose a piece after ...h2.

TWO BISHOPS OR TIME?

EVANS—LARSEN

U.S. Open Championship 1949

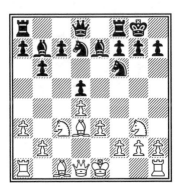

Diagram 82

White moves. Granted that two bishops are preferable in the majority of positions, just how much is it worth going out of one's way to win them? Is it worth neglect of development and loss of Time? The answer clearly depends on the given position. As a general rule, Time is more important in open games; in closed games it's easier to delay development without paying a heavy price.

1 Nf5. The specific problem is whether White should castle or move this already developed piece in order to swap it for a bishop. The order of moves is more than academic. If 1 0-0 Re8 2 Nf5 Bf8 saves the bishop which serves a valuable function by guarding the dark squares. Since the position is sufficiently closed, White can afford to move his knight in order to "win" the bishop. Others may disagree, but the course of the game justified this strategy. **Re8 2 Nxe7+ Qxe7 3 0-0 c5 4 b4 c4.** If instead 4...cxb4 5 cxb4 Qxb4 6 Nb5! threatens Nc7 and/or Ba3. Black now has established a protected passed c-pawn which is ordinarily a strong formation. White's compensation is the two bishops plus the possibility of mobilizing his central majority by f3 and e4. See Diagram 23 (p. 47) for later developments.

FORCE OR TIME?

KATZ—EVANS

Diagram 83

White moves. Many positions pose a real dilemma: Repair Force and lose Time, or repair Time and lose Force? There is no blanket answer. The general rule is that Force is more important than Time in the long run and should be given preference in the absence of any other vital considerations.

1 Nxd4. The question is whether White should castle or capture this pawn. He fears that 1 0-0 Bc5 will hold the pawn, so he decides to repair Force even though it means he must move his king in the sequence. Note that 1...Qxd4?? 2 Bxb5+ axb5 3 Qxd4 costs Black his queen. **Bb4+ 2 Kf1 Qd5 3 Nf3 Bb7 4 a3 Bc5 5 h3 0–0.** Black has a splendid aggressive lineup against White's hapless king. Play continued: **6 Be5 Ne4 7 Bxe4 Qxe4 8 Qe2 Qf5** with an abiding attack that carried the day.

SNATCH PAWNS— ONLY IF YOU CAN SURVIVE!

BISGUIER—SHERWIN

New York 1955

Diagram 84

Black moves. Scavenging for material while neglecting development is a typical beginner's mistake. White just played Nc3 inviting Qxb2. Black can ignore this gift by continuing his development with the placid Be7 or accept the challenge by plunging his queen into dangerous depths. He takes the plunge and lives to tell the tale!

1...Qxb2. Chess lore has a standing taboo against this kind of capture at the cost of development. As he made his move Sherwin quipped, "Why should I labor under antediluvian prejudices?" Bisguier smiled enigmatically. The test for snatching material is whether you see how to get away with it, even if it means undergoing an arduous defense before your advantage in Force begins to manifest itself. **2 Nb5 Qb4+ 3 c3 Qa5.** Returning quickly to stop Nc7+. **4 Nd2 a6!** A magnificent conception. An alternate defense is 4...d5 5 Bf4 Na6 7 dxc5 Bxc5 8 Nxc5 Qxc5 9 Bd6 when Black is a pawn up but will have trouble castling. **5 Nc4 Qxb5!** The point. Not 5...Qd8? 6 Nbd6+ Bxd6 7 Nxd6+ Ke7 8 dxc5 regaining the pawn while Black's king is stranded in the center. **6 Nd6+ Bxd6 7 Bxb5 axb5.** Time to take reckoning. Black has three minor pieces for the queen, more than enough, and won after he succeeded in consolidating.

TO TAKE OR NOT TO TAKE

EVANS—SUSSMAN

New York 1950

Diagram 85

White moves. Black has a formidable attack after sacrificing his bishop for a pawn on h3. White can capture the knight or the bishop, but neither one looks appetizing in view of his exposed king. Declining the offer by 1 Qg3 Qh5 2 Nc3 f5 3 gxh3 Nxh3+ 4 Kg2 Nxf4+ 5 Rxf4 Bxf4 6 Qxf4 seems prudent, and so does 1 Rf2.

If a sacrifice is unsound, then naturally it should be accepted. If it is sound, then it can't be refuted. In time pressure I foolishly chose **1 gxh3?** Even worse is 1 fxg5? Bxg2! 2 Kxg2 Qh2+ 3 Kf3 Qh3+ (or 3...Rxe2) 4 Kf2 Qxd3. **Nxh3+ 2 Kg2 Qg4+ 3 Ng3 Nxf4+ 4 Rxf4 Bxf4 5 Qf3 Re2+?** Returning the favor.

Simply 3...Qg5 or Qxf3+ should win. 6 **Qxe2 Qxg3+ 7 Kf1 Qh3+ 8 Qg2 Qd3+ 9 Kg1 Re8??** This monstrous blunder is explicable only by the fact that Black had only seconds left to the time control but it's bad in any event after 9...g6 10 Rf1 Rc8 11 Qf3. **7 Qxg7 mate.** Sometimes it's better to be lucky than good.

THE SWORD OF DAMOCLES

EVANS—HANAUER

U.S. Championship 1951

Diagram 86

White moves. Force can often be used to win more Force! White would win easily with his extra pawn if he could swap rooks, and this constant threat hanging over Black's head permits White to gain Time and make further inroads. We like to think of this process as the sword of Damocles, a Greek legend that is a somber reminder of imminent peril.

1 Re1. Watch how this rook gradually gains Space by threatening to invade on e7. White wants to exchange all the pieces or at least rook for rook, hence he abstains from 1 a4 Nc7 2 Bxc7 Kxc7 giving Black drawing chances in the rook and pawn ending. White has no intention of swapping bishop for knight just yet! **Rf7 2 Re5! a6.** Not 2...Nc7 3 Rc5 swapping all the pieces and leaving White with an easily won king and pawn ending. **3 Rc5+ Kd8 4 Bb8.** A study in technique. The bishop takes the retreat at a7 away from the knight and the threat of a4 compels Black to weaken his Pawn Structure. **b6 5 Rc6 Rb7 6 Bf4 Kd7 7 Rc4 Na7 8 Be3 Nc6 9 Rh4!** Provoking further pawn weaknesses. Notice how White operates with threats on both sides of the board. **h6 10 Rg4 Na5+ 11 Ka4 Kc6 12 Rg6+ Kd5 13 Rxb6.** Winning a second pawn and the game came tumbling after. It concluded: **13...Rxb6 14 Bxb6 Nc4 15 Bd4 g6 16 Kb4 h5 17 h4 Nd6 18 Ka5 Nf5 19 g3 1-0.**

CONVERTING FORCE INTO SPACE

EVANS—STEINER

3rd match game 1952

Diagram 87

White moves. There is an old saying that the hardest thing in chess is to win a won game. White is an Exchange ahead but Black dominates Space and has the initiative. The key principle here is that White's advantage in Force automatically confers an advantage in Time because *each swap benefits the stronger side.*

1 Ra5! Qc3. 1...Qxa5 2 Qxe3 would ease White's defensive task. Black's only chance is to try and keep it complicated. The threat of ...Re2 is gone now that the queen has been ousted from its post on e5. **2 Rc4! Qa3.** Once again White utilizes the offer to swap rooks to gain Space and drive the queen still further out of play. **3 Rb5.** White's rooks are coordinated and the rest, though difficult, is a matter of technique. The a-pawn is the decisive factor and without it the game would be equal. Here are the remaining moves: **Kh7 4 Be4! Kh6 5 Bxg6 fxg6 6 Qf6 Ng7 7 Rc7 Qa2+ 8 Kh3 Qe6+ 9 Qxe6 Nxe6 10 Rc4 Re2 11 g4 Re3+ 12 Kg2 h4 13 g5+ Kh5 14 Rbb4 h3+ 15 Kh2 Kxg5 16 Rh4 Kf5 17 Rxh3 Re2+ 18 Kg1 g5 19 Ra3 g5 20 a5** (finally this pawn starts marching) **Ng5 21 a6 Nf3+ 22 Kf1 Rh2 23 a7 Rh1+** (a spite check!) **24 Kf2 1-0.**

SIMPLIFICATION

EVANS—LYMAN

Hollywood 1954

Diagram 88

White moves. Simplification is a valuable defensive resource. Each exchange eases the task of the defender because there is one less attacking piece to worry about. As in the previous example, White is an Exchange ahead but the terrible knights threaten to ride roughshod over him. The immediate threat is ...Nxc3. If 1 Rxd5? Qb1+ 2 Kf2 Qxa2+ wins. Clearly forceful tactics are required to blunt Black's initiative.

1 f5! This clearance sacrifice gives the bishop more scope. Because White is ahead in material, he can afford to relinquish this pawn to ease pressure. **Rxf5.** After 1...Qxf5 2 Qxf5 Rxf5 3 Bd4 gets the queens off the board. If now 3...Nxd4 4 Rxd4 Nxc3 Rc2. **2 Rxd5!** The point is Black no longer has Qb1+ because he blocked this diagonal with his rook. **Rxd5 3 Qc8+ Kf7 6 Rf2+ Ke7.** White returned the Exchange and is a pawn down to boot but his ferocious attack carried the day after 7 **Qf8+** (7 Qxc4? Rd1+ 8 Rf1 Rxf1+ 9 Qxf1 is only equal).

WHEN EQUAL FORCE ISN'T EQUAL

BERLINER—EVANS

U.S. Open Championship 1950

Diagram 89

Black moves. Only one knight has been exchanged and material is equal. However, this is a mirage. Upon closer examination the bishop on h1 is hemmed without an exit. In effect, White is a piece down and his position disintegrates after Black rips open the queenside.

1...b6! 2 c2 a5! 3 a3 axb4 4 axb4 Ba6 5 Rfc1 Bb5 6 Rxa8 Qxa8 7 Ra1 Qb7 8 Ra3 Ra8 9 Qc3 Bf6 10 Rxa8 Qxa8 11 Qa3 Qxa3 12 Bxa3 bxc5 13 bxc5 Kf7. Starting a long march to the other wing. The king is a fighting piece—use it! **14 Nb1 Ke8 15 Ke1 Kd8 16 Kd2 Kc7 17 Bb4 Kb7 18 Na3 Bd8.** It's too soon for 18...Bf1 19 Ke1 Bg2? 20 Bxg2 hxg2 21 Kf2 but White constantly must guard against this threat. **19 Ke1 Ka6 20 Nb1 Ba5 21 Bxa5 Kxa5 22 Nd2 Kb4 23 Bf3.** Desperation. The bishop is useless anyway. **gxf3 24 Nxf3 Nf6.** Black won easily with his extra piece. Notice how logically he penetrated via the open lines created on the queenside to free the bishop on c8.

THE BEST DEFENSE IS ATTACK

SANTASIERE—EVANS

U.S. Championship 1948

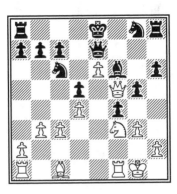

Diagram 90

Black moves. He is a piece ahead but his pieces are undeveloped and his king already has moved, thus forfeiting the privilege of castling. White threatens to tear open the f-file in order to get at Black's exposed king. Should Black be tightfisted or liberal? The principle involved in defending is to return a few pawns in order to bring pieces into play. *Extra material is worthless unless it can be used!*

1...Qh7 Better is 1...fxg3 2 hxg3 Qd6 3 Kg2 Nce7 but I prefer active defense. This is no time for tightfisted moves like 1...Rd8 2 Qg6+ Kf8 3 Ba3! Rd6 (not 3...Qxa3 4 Qf7 mate) 4 gxf4 with good counterplay. **2 Qxd5 Rd8 3 Qb5 Nge7.** Getting another piece out without worrying about protecting the pawn on b7. **4 gxf4 gxf4 5 Bxf4 Rg8+ 6 Kh1 Rd5.** This rook did nothing in the diagram but now comes strongly into play. 7 **Qxb7 Qc2 8 Nd2 Qxc3 9 Rac1 Qh3.** Again threatening Qg2 mate. In return for giving up a bunch of pawns Black has seized the initiative but now gets it all back with dividends. **10 Rg1 Rxg1+ 11 Rxg1 Qxe6.** White's attack has been repulsed, his king is exposed, and Black is still a piece up. The game concluded: **12 Qa6 Rxd4 13 Qf1 Qd5+ 14 Rg2 Bg5 15 Bxg5 hxg5 16 Qe2 g4 17 Kg1 Ne5 18 Nf1 Nf3+ 19 Kf2 Rf4 20 Ne3 Nd4+ 0–1**

THE POSITIONAL SACRIFICE

The consequences of a positional sacrifice are supposed to unfold gradually, as in a Greek drama. The outcome is not always immediately apparent and often the only tangible return is pressure. Sometimes the motive is so murky that one is tempted to wonder whether the sacrifice is intentional. At Carlsbad 1907 Cohn was awarded the brilliancy prize against Tchigorin for "a beautiful combination starting from an extraordinary deep pawn sacrifice." But after the game Cohn admitted he had not intended to sacrifice the pawn—he lost it, after which he had been forced to play energetically to compensate for his material deficit!

The following example of a pure positional sacrifice in the Najdorf Variation of the Sicilian Defense had a strange genesis: **1 e4 c5 2 Nf3 d6 3 d4 cxd4 4 Nxd4 Nf6 5 Nc3 a6 6 Bg5 e6 7 f4 Be7 8 Qf3 h6 9 Bh4 g5!? 10 fxg5.**

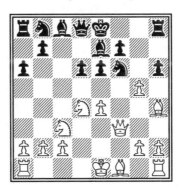

Diagram 91

This position saw the light of day in 1955 at Gothenburg, Sweden, when three Argentinians faced three Russians in the same round and sprang this prepared variation. All three games continued with **10...Nfd7** and Black lost with dispatch after **11 Nxe6! fxe6 12 Qh5+ Kf8 13 Bb5!** The point is 13... axb5 loses to 14 0-0+ Bf6 15e5! dxe5 16 Ne4. Geller-Panno continued: 13...Ne5 14 Bg3! Bxg5 15 0-0+ Ke7 16 Bxe5 Qb6+ 17 Kh1 dxe5 18 Qf7+ Kd6 19 Rad1+ Qd4 20 Rxd4+ exd4 21 e5+ Kc5 22 Qc7+ Nc6 23 Bxc6 1-0.

It has since been found that **13...Rh7!** holds.

After this triple massacre Panno, Pilnik and Najdorf went back to the workshop and came up with **10...hxg5 11 Bxg5 Nbd7** which is a positional sacrifice in the finest sense of the word because Black seemingly gave up a pawn and smashed his own kingside without sufficient compensation.

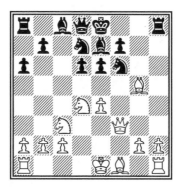

Diagram 92

Black has a compact pawn mass in the center, has gained e5 for his knight, and controls open lines on the kingside. Since then tournament practice and computers decided that it's insufficient compensation for the pawn after, for example, 12 0-0-0 Ne5 13 Qe2.

The major criterion for a positional sacrifice is that it be *intentional.* The rest is a matter of judgment. Unlike the temporary sacrifice, whose aim is well-defined, the positional sacrifice has no clear-cut purpose and the result lies in the lap of the gods.

THE TEMPORARY SACRIFICE

Unlike the positional sacrifice, the temporary one has an immediate and tangible end. In his excellent book, *The Art of Sacrifice in Chess,* Rudolph Spielmann points out two kinds of temporary tactical sacs: (1) the sacrifice for gain; (2) the mating sacrifice.

(1) THE SACRIFICE FOR GAIN

Ruy Lopez. **1 e4 e5 2 Nf3 Nc6 3 Bb5 a6 4 Ba4 Nf6 5 0-0 Be7 6 d4 b5 7 Bb3 Nxd4?** Correct is 7...exd4. **8 Bxf7+!**

Black was hoping to catch White in the Noah's Ark Trap after 8 Nxd4 exd4 9 Qxd4 c5 followed by c4 but this crosses him up.

Diagram 93

Kxf7 9 Nxe5+ Kf8. Even worse is 9...Ke6 10 Qxd4 c5 11 Qc3 Nxe4 12 Qf3 Kxe5 13 Bf4+ Kd5 14 Re1 Kc6 15 Qxe4+ d5 16 Qxe7. **10 Qxd4.** White has regained his piece with interest and Black can no longer castle.

(2) THE MATING SACRIFICE

Philidor Defense. 1 e4 e5 2 Nf3 d6 3 Bc4 h6 4 Nc3 Nc6 5 d4 Bg4 6 dxe5 Nxe5? 7 Nxe5!

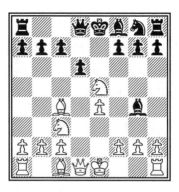

Diagram 94

If 7...Bxd1? 8 Bxf7+ Ke7 9 Nd5 mate. The mate can be averted by 7...dxe5 but White merely remains a piece ahead after 8 Qxg4.

CONCEPTS IN FORCE

PIECE VS. THREE PAWNS

EVANS—KRAMER

New York 1951

Diagram 95

White moves. In the middle game a piece is usually better than three pawns. In the endgame, owing to its unique queening power, a pawn increase in value. This position is instructive, difficult and roughly equal. If Black can mobilize his pawns, he will have winning chances. But for now the pawns are relatively static.

1 Rhe1 e5. This push prematurely weakens the light squares. Building up in the center with 1...Rhe8 is more prudent. In order to preserve winning chances, White must keep most of his pawns on the board. The immediate plan is to restrain Black's center and punch weaknesses in what is now a sound Pawn Structure. **2 Rad1 Kc7 3 Nc5 Rhe8 4 Re2 b6 5 axb6+ axb6 6 Na6+ Kb7 7 Red2 b5?** The losing move. 7...Rc8 8 Nb4 Nxb4 9 Kxb4 is still a hard fight. **8 Bxb5! cxb5 9 Nb4 Nxb4.** Black must either sacrifice the Exchange (which he does) or wind up with only two pawns for the piece. **10 Rxd8 Rxd8 11 Rxd8 Kc7 12 Rg8 Nd3 13 Rxg7+ Kd6 14 Kc3 e4 15 Rxh7 Ke5 16 Rh5+ f5 17 g4 b4+ 18 Kd2 Nxb2 19 Rxf5+ Kd4 20 g5.** The rest is easy now that the passed pawns start moving..

QUEEN VS. UNCOORDINATED MINOR PIECES

KRAMER—EVANS

New York 1949

Diagram 96

White moves. Theoretically White has material equality with two rooks for a queen—100 units to 100 units. But here his pieces are so uncoordinated and Black's knights so intimidating that White is likely to lose a piece trying to consolidate. The immediate threat is 1...Nxc1 2 Rxc1 Qxb5. In order to meet this threat, White drops a piece anyway.

1 **Nc3.** No better is 1 Bg5 Qd5 2 h4 h6 3 Rd8 Qc6 4 Be7 Ne3 5 d5 Qc2. **Qd7 2 Re4.** To stop Qxd4+. f5 **3 Rh4 f4!** **4 Ne2 Qe7 0-1.** White can't meet the double threat of Qxh4 or Qxe2.

QUEEN VS. COORDINATED MINOR PIECES

HEARST—EVANS_____

U.S. Championship 1954

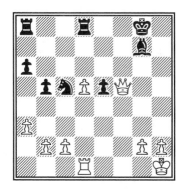

Diagram 97

Black moves. At first glance this is difficult to evaluate. White has a queen plus three pawns for a rook and two pieces—130 to 120 units in his favor on the table of relative values. As a general rule the pieces are preferable *if* they can coordinate and penetrate before the pawns advance far enough to do much harm. So the pieces must be made aggressive at all cost.

1...Rxd5? Short of time, I panicked and walked into a lost ending. The best defense is 1...Rd6! Also tough is 1...Rf8 2 Qh3 Ne4 3 Qe6+ Kh8 4 Kg1. **2 Rxd5 Rf8 3 Qxf8+ Bxf8 4 Rxe5.** White won because the minor pieces are no match for the pawns.

119

QUEEN VS. TWO ROOKS

NAJDORF—EVANS

Cuba 1952

Diagram 98

Draw Agreed. This is the usual case. White is a pawn ahead but can't make progress because the rooks are connected and maintain an invulnerable blockade on their rank. Even if White succeeds in creating a passed pawn on the queenside it cannot break the blockade. White enjoys a theoretical advantage of 110 to 100 units, but he can't make headway.

Moral: Connect your rooks!

SPACE

When two experts are evenly matched it's unlikely that either one will lose material in the opening. Nor is it likely that one of them will ruin his Pawn Structure or fall too far behind in development (although failure to castle early is still a leading cause of disaster). As a rule, however, White will acquire a spatial advantage thanks to moving first, which is akin to the serve in tennis. Once this initiative evaporates, Black achieves equality.

Space refers to the area controlled or occupied by each army beyond the fourth rank—the frontier line.

THE FRONTIER LINE

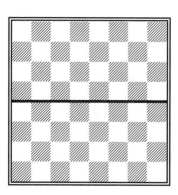

Diagram 99

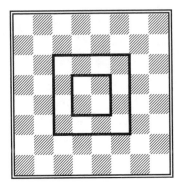

Diagram 100

12 SQUARE CENTER

The center is crucial and should be regarded as the core of the chessboard. The idea behind the opening is develop your pieces as fast as possible and castle early to safeguard your king.

Work towards the middle! When pieces or pawns are placed in or near the center their mobility increases. By controlling or occupying the center you cramp your opponent and force him to station his troops on inferior squares.

MOBILITY

Mobility means freedom of movement. When pieces occupy the center, they radiate greater mobility. For example, consider a white knight on f3 opposed to a black knight on a6. White's knight is stronger. The one on f3 strikes at eight squares, whereas its counterpart on a6 strikes at only four squares. The same applies to the other pieces, proportionate to their distance from the center.

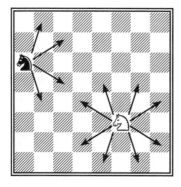

Diagram 101

CONTROLLING UNOCCUPIED SQUARES

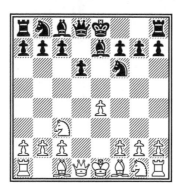

Diagram 102

White has a spatial edge. White temporarily controls d5, a key central square even though it's unoccupied. Black's bishop on e7 is confined to a dead diagonal unless he advances his pawn to d5. At the moment White observes d5 three times (with pawn, knight and queen) so in order to enforce ...d5 Black must first bring an additional unit to bear on that square

123

by Be6 or c6 or both. The conflict from here clearly will revolve around Black's constant challenge in the center vs. White's attempt to maintain control of d5.

A TYPICAL SPACE ADVANTAGE

In the following variation of the Nimzo-Indian Defense White controls d5 in a different way—by occupying it: **1 d4 Nf6 2 c4 e6 3 Nc3 Bb4 4 e3 b6 5 Nge2 Bb7 6 a3 Be7 7 d5 0–0 8 g3 d6 9 Bg2 e5 10 0–0 Nbd7 11 e4.**

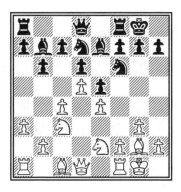

Diagram 103

Black is cramped. White has a strong wedge of pawns in the center. Black can try for counterplay by 11...Ne8 followed by g6 and f5 but this still won't free his game or empower his bishops. In fact, after 11...c6? 12 dxc6 Bxc6 Black will have a glaring backward d-pawn on an open file.

The immediate 11...Ba6 is met simply by 12 b3. Another plan is 11...a5 intending Nc5, a4 and Ba6 to artificially isolate the pawn on c4, but this is slow and can be thwarted by 12 Rb1 Nc5 13 b4 axb4 14 axb4. A positional player might try to strangle Black slowly to death, whereas a tactician might opt for the double-edged f4.

HOW TO COUNT SPACE

In Diagram 103 Black strikes at four empty squares past his fourth rank (d4 and f4 with his e-pawn; e4 and g4 with his knight). White occupies one square (d5) and strikes at seven (b5 with his knight; g5 and h6 with his bishop; b5, c6, e6, f5 with his pawns). Thus White has an 8 to 4 advantage in Space.

STABILITY

It's not enough merely to control or occupy Space—you must be able to retain it! Invasion or penetration by itself means little unless the advanced troops can be maintained with a steady line of communication and a steady flow of supplies and reinforcements. Napoleon's *grande armée* is stranded in the Russian campaign has its counterpart in an overextended center. As we saw in a previous chapter, this question was tossed into the theoretical cauldron by the Hypermoderns, yet there are definite ways to test stability.

HOW TO TEST STABILITY

In the Sicilian Defense **1 e4 c5 2 Nf3 Nc6 3 g3 Nf6 4 e5?** is premature. It can be refuted by **Ng4!**

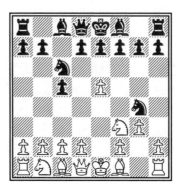

Diagram 104

Pity the pawn on e5. The artificially isolated pawn on e5 is attacked twice, protected once, and will fall. The test of stability depends upon whether the support for an advanced outpost exceeds the means by which it can be assailed. No help is 5 Qe2 Qc7 devouring the advanced pawn. White also can try to maintain this outpost by tactical means: 5 d4 cxd4 6 Bf4 but now 6...Ngxe5! 7 Nxe5 Nxe5 8 Bxe5 Qa5+ 5 Nd2 Qxe5+ snares a second pawn and the rest is a matter of technique. As one wag quipped: "Pawns are like buttons. Lose too many and the pants fall down by themselves."

Let's tackle a more complex problem, the Yugoslav Variation of the King's Indian Defense: 1 d4 Nf6 2 c4 g6 3 Nc3 Bg7 4 g3 0-0 5 Bg2 d6 6 Nf3 c5 7 d5.

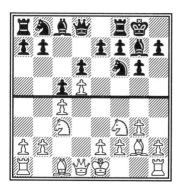

Diagram 105

Can White maintain his center? To answer this question, we first must investigate how Black can undermine this seemingly formidable center. What we really want to know is whether the pawn on d5 is an asset or a liability. Before going into that, note that White has a slight edge in Space (by count 8 to 6).

Black has four plausible moves. The first one that leaps to mind is 7...e6 for after 8 dxe6 Bxe6 (if 8...fxe6 9 e4 keeps the edge) Black attacks c4 and prepares ...d5 but White stays on top with 9 Ng5! (9...Bxc4? 10 Bxb7). Another try is 7...a6 8 0-0 Bd7 9 a4 and Black will have a hard time freeing his game with ...b5. And if 7...Bg4 8 0-0 Nbd7 (better than 8...Bxf3 9 exf3! Nbd7 10 Re1) 9 Nd2! Nb6 10 h3 Bd7 11 e4 Black remains cramped.

Finally, Black can try to undermine the center from the flank by 7...Na6. The point is to reinforce ...b5 by retreating the knight to c7 before playing a6. The game might continue 8 0-0 Nc7 9 e4 a6 10 a4 confronting Black with two alternatives. A. 10...Rb8 11 a5 b5 12 axb6 Rxb6 with pressure along the b-file but with little hope of assailing the center after 13 Re1. B. 10...b6 (inviting 11 a5? b5) 11 Re1 Rb8 12 e5! Nd7 13 Bf4 with pressure in the center before Black can retaliate with ...b5.

Thus the answer to the question is yes. White can maintain his center because Time is a crucial factor in his favor. If Black's knight were already on c7 instead of b8, then White's center would be much weaker.

CONCEPTS IN SPACE

CENTRALIZE KINGS IN THE ENDGAME

EVANS–KÖNIG

Hastings 1949-50

Diagram 106

Black moves. An advantage in Space is surprisingly enduring. Despite the reduction in forces, White wins because his men are better placed. Even without knights, he would win the king and pawn ending. The centralization of White's king beyond The Frontier Line can be converted into material gain.

1...Nc4. Trying to activate the knight. The b-pawn is doomed anyway after 1...Kd7 2 Kc5. White must now be careful to avoid the trap of 2 Nxb5? Ne3+ 3 Ke4 Nc2 4 Nc3 Nxb4 5 Nd5+ Nxd5 6 Kxd5 Kd7 keeping the opposition which draws. 2 Kc5! **Ne3 3 Kc6 Kd8 4 Kxb5 Kc7 5 Ka6 Nc4 6 b5 Kd6 7 b6 Ne5 8 b7 Nd7 9 Ne6 1-0.** The pawn queens on 9... Ke5 10 Ka7 Kxf5 11 Nf8 Nxf8 12 b8/Q.

Moral: In the endgame the king is a fighting piece. Use it!

DON'T HEM IN YOUR BISHOPS

Diagram 107
Position after 3...Nf6

White moves. A typical example of developing bishops before pushing the e-pawn arises in the Queen's Gambit Declined after 1 d4 d5 2 c4 e6 3 Nc3 Nf6. White now has a choice between 4 e3 or Bg5. He should develop the bishop first so as not to lock it in.

The principle of mobility is involved. Bishops are less effective behind closed lines, and only in case of necessity should we voluntarily hem them in with our own pawns. In this defense Black's bishop on c8 is known as "the problem child" because developing it is difficult. The drawback of declining the gambit with 2...e6 is that this bishop must eventually be freed either by placing it on b7 or by striving for ...e5. Black is cramped and will remain passive for quite a while after 3 Bg5 exerting indirect pressure on d5 (also playable but less logical is 3 Bf4).

The Slav Defense is one way to decline the gambit without locking in the bishop on c8: 1 d4 d5 2 c4 c6 3 Nf3 Nf6 4 Nc3 dxc4 5 a4 (to regain the pawn by preventing ...b5) Bf5 6 e3 e6

7 Bxc4 Bb4 8 0-0 0-0 and Black has freed both his bishops. The Queen's Gambit Accepted is another acceptable way to free the bishops: 1 d4 d5 2 c4 dxc4 3 Nf3 Nf6 4 e3 a6 5 Bxc4 e6 6 0-0 c5 (see diagram 111 (p. 133)).

Both of these alternatives are satisfactory, depending upon which one fits your style and makes you feel more comfortable. Both, however, have the drawback of letting White get in an early e4.

RESTRAIN KEY FREEING MOVES

NIMZO—INDIAN DEFENSE

Diagram 108
Position after 3...Bb4

White moves. Restraint is a method of preventing moves that permit your opponent to expand. The Nimzo-Indian Defense (named in honor of Aaron Nimzovich) is a good example of what its founder termed "prophylaxis" or, as I prefer to call it, restraint. It arises after **1 d4 Nf6 2 c4 e6 3 Nc3 Bb4.**

Black's last move develops a piece, initiates an annoying pin, prepares castling and—just as importantly—stops White from expanding with e4. The most popular reply is 4 e3 hemming in the bishop on c1. Trying to bring it out first by 4 Bg5 (a favorite of Spassky) can be met by 4...g5 Bg3 Ne4. Every move in the world has been tried here for White, yet still no way has been found to secure more than a minimal edge. Offhand 4 f3 looks feasible, but it takes the best square away from the knight on g1 and is adequately met by 4...d5 without fearing 5 Qa4+ Nc6.

WHEN TO DECENTRALIZE

Diagram 109
Sicilian Defense

White moves. He has a minimal Space advantage in this so-called Dragon Variation. It's important to stop Black from freeing his game with ...d5 even if it means losing a tempo by 1 Nb3! in order to observe d5 with his queen. The fight might continue 1...Be6 2 f4 and now Black will have to seek moves such as Na5 or Qd7 since 2...d5?! is dubious in view of 3 f5. Let's see why theory prefers the paradoxical retreat 1 Nb3! over the alternatives.

- **A.** 1 Qd2 d5 Also satisfactory is 1...Ng4. 2 exd5 No better is 2 Nxc6 bxc6 3 e5 Ng4. 2 exd5 Nxd5 3 Nxd5 Nxd4! 4 Bxd4 Qxd5 and Black has freed his game with full equality.
- **B.** 1 Bf3. An awkward way to stop ...d5 that blocks f4. Bd7. Black harmoniously completes his development. Also note that 1...Ne5 2 Be2 Nc6

3 Bf3 Ne5 could lead to a draw by repetition if White doesn't want to part with his two bishops by allowing Nxf3+.

C. **1 Nxc6?! bxc6 2 Bf3 Rb8 3 Rb1 Qa5** and Black seize the initiative.

D. **1 f4 Ng4!** More complicated but playable is 1... Qb6. **2 Bxg4.** Black is fine after 2 Nxc6 Nxe3 3 Nxd8 Nxd1 4 Raxd1 Rxd8 5 Nd5 Kf8 6 c3 Bd7. **Bxd4! 3 Bxd4 Bxg4 4 Qxg4 Nxd4 5 Qd1 Nc6** lets Black simplify too soon by releasing the tension.

RESTRAINING THE MINORITY ATTACK

D. BYRNE—EVANS
New York 1955

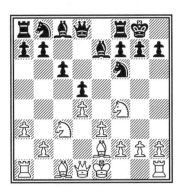

Diagram 110

Black moves. White exerts pressure on d5 and wants to weaken its base by b4 and b5—the minority attack (see Diagram 75 (p. 93)). By the simple expedient of **1...a5!** Black can frustrate this plan or make it very difficult to implement. It's true that this move creates a hole at b6, but it would be weakened anyway after the inevitable ...a6. So the choice is really between a passive or an aggressive pawn formation. Sometimes is pays to lose a tempo in order to restrain a maneuver that would cost far more time to stop once it gets started.

The game continued: **2 0-0 Re8 3 f3 Bf8.** This innocuous retreat stops White from expanding with e4. It's often more important to frustrate your opponent's plans than to be obsessed with your own sly designs. **4 Rb1.** Faulty strategy. White wants to prepare b4 and continue with the minority attack, but he hasn't got enough time to succeed with two ideas at once. Better is 4 Bd3. **Bf5 5 Nd3 h6.** Black has freedom for all his pieces, and his last move was designed to make an escape square for the bishop at h7 in case it's attacked by g4. Note that White now stands worse because he hasn't solved the problem of opening lines for his bishop on c1.

DOUBLE-EDGED RESTRAINING MOVES

Diagram 111
Queen's Gambit Accepted, Position after 6 a4

Black moves. In this opening after **1 d4 d5 2 c4 dxc4 3 Nf3 Nf6 4 e3 e6 5 Bxc4 a6** experience has shown that White does better to castle and let Black to expand with ...b5 than to try and restrain it with **6 a4.** Why?

The principle behind White's last move is good: restraint. But it creates a hole on b4 which can't be repaired. In other words, restraining moves are good only if they serve a function without fundamentally weakening the Pawn Structure. You must always keep the long-range prospect of the endgame in mind. Reshevsky-Fine, Semmering 1937, continued: **6...c5 7 0-0 Nc6 8 Nc3 Be7.** It's true that Black can't develop his bishop on c8 with ease, but on the other hand White has the same trouble developing his bishop on c1, and he has weakened his weak Pawn Structure to boot. **9 Qe2 0–0 10 Rd1 Qc7 11 h3 Rd8 12 d5 exd5 13 Bxd5 Nb4** with equality.

THE BIND

EVANS—HOWARD_____

New York 1948

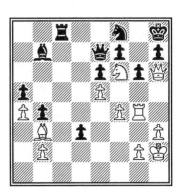

Diagram 112

Black moves. A bind is a stranglehold (see also Diagram 70). It usually occurs after one player has acquired a weak square complex, and this is a drastic example. Black's dark kingside squares are hopelessly feeble and he can't meet the threat of Rh4 and Qxh7+. A bit pat, perhaps, but not if it gets across the point that constriction is bad for your health.

1...Be4. Desperation, hoping to meet 2 Rh4 by g5. The only other attempt at counterplay was 1...Rc2 but 2 Bxc2 dxc2 3 Rh4 c1/Q 4 Qxh7+ Nxh7 5 Rxh7 mate. **2 Nxe4 1-0.** White won a piece and renews the threat of Nf6 and Rh4. With proper play, nobody should be able to tie you up so completely.

FIGHT A BIND!

EVANS–BARDA

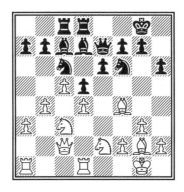

Diagram 113

Black moves. Violent measures, even sacrifice, must be considered in order to shake off the far-reaching tentacles of a bind while there is still time. White threatens to gradually smother Black by an oncoming mass of queenside pawns. Instead of a passive move like 1...a6 Black tries to shake free with **1...e5!?** That this costs the pawn on d5 is of relatively little moment. The important thing is to play it while he can still breathe and profit tactically from the open lines. **2 dxe5 Nxe5 3 Nxd5 Nxd5 4 Rxd5 Bg4 5 Rxd8+ Rxd8 6 Bxe5.** Squelching threats against the hole on f3 once and for all. Grabbing another pawn by 6 Bxb7! looks dangerous but is quite playable. **Bxe5.** No better is 6...Qxe5 7 Nc3 Bf5 8 Qc1.

7 Re1 Bf6 8 h3. A handy way to make "*luft*" on h2 with gain of tempo. **Bh5 9 Qe4 Qxe4 10 Bxe4 Re8 11 Nf4?** Correct is 11 f3. **Bf3 12 Bh7+ Kf8 13 Rxe8+ Kxe8 14 Bc2 Bb2 15 a4 Draw.** After 15...Ba3 16 Nd3 Be4 17 b5 Bxd3 18 Bxd3 Bxc5 regains the pawn with opposite colored bishops.

WHEN CRAMPED, SWAP PIECES

ROTHMAN—EVANS_____

New York 1948

Diagram 114

Black moves. Swaps provide elbow room. Sometimes we must adopt apparently outlandish measures in order to shake free of a cramp. White's backward pawn on d4 is a glaring weakness, but how to get at it? Black is reluctant to castle into a fierce attack after 1...0-0 h5 but doesn't want to keep his king in the center either. Quite a conundrum. What to do?

The solution is **1...Bb4+!** taking advantage of the pin on the a-file to swap bishops and free e7 to maneuver his pieces. **2 Bd2 Bxd2+.** Gladly! **3 Qxd2 Ne7!** Headed for f5 or d5 as circumstances demand. **4 Bd3 Bc6 5 Rg3 g6.** Black has relieved his cramp and obtained freedom of movement. If now 6 Qh6 Bxf3 7 Rxf3 Qxd4 8 Qg7 Rf8 easily rebuffs the attack.

FREEING COMBINATIONS

DONOVAN—EVANS

Diagram 115

Black moves. Cramped positions sometimes are resilient and one move often can bring the sleeping pieces all to life. White has a Space advantage but his overextended central pawns could become burdensome. The freeing principle consists in striking at the center from the flank.

1...c5! Converting Time (the move) into Space to rip White's center to shreds. **2 0-0?** A speculative pawn sacrifice. Better is 1 Qe2! cxd4 2 Bxd4 keeping Black bottled up. **cxd4 3 Bxd4 dxe5 4 fxe5 Nxe5! 5 Bxe5 Bxe5 6 Nxe5 Qd4+ 7 Kh1 Qxe5.** White has some pressure but not enough compensation for a pawn.

REBUFFING FLANK ATTACKS

KAGETSU—EVANS_____

Hollywood 1954

Diagram 116

Black moves. The attacker doesn't always benefit from open lines and, if possible, should close the center before embarking on a wing attack. The defender must keep lines of communication fluid in order to divert his pieces from the other flank to help his endangered king. Black is a rook ahead but is skating on thin ice and he would be in grave peril were White on move: 1 Qxh1 Bb7 2 Qf3 f5 3 Qh5 Bf6 4 0–0–0 fxe4 5 Qh7+ Kf8 6 Nh5.

1...d5! It turns out that 1...Bb7 (or f5) 2 Qxh1 f5 is even better, but in the heat of battle I thought Black must somehow be able to play Qxh3 to blunt the attack. To do this, the knight on f4 must be dislodged by shifting the bishop to d6. Via this chain of reasoning, I arrived at the general principle that a wing attack is best met by a reaction in the center. The text frees d6 for the bishop. **2 Qxh1 Bd6 3 0–0–0.** White has no time for 3 Qf3 dxe4 4 Bxe4 Bxf4 5 Bxf4 (or 5 Qxf4 Bb7) Qd4! and wins. **Rb7!?** Good enough but stronger is 3...d4. Finally the pressure is off and the object of this "mysterious" rook move is not so mysterious. If 4 Qxf3 Bxf4 5 Bxf4 Qxh3 and the rook on b8 no longer is exposed to capture. Now it's all over except for the handshake and Black quickly whipped up a crushing counterattack after **4 h4 Bxf4 5 Bxf4 Qg4 6 Bd2 dxe4 7 Rg1 Qe6 8 Be2 Qa2!**

CONNECT YOUR ROOKS

FLEISCHER—EVANS

U.S. Open 1949

Diagram 117

Black moves. This principle is very simple. It merely states that the goal of development is to clear all your pieces off the first rank until the rooks are connected. In this way both rooks can occupy any open files, especially in the center. When this happens, it usually heralds the end of the opening and the beginning of the middle game.

1...Bd7! Using the lull to connect rooks. **2 Qb3.** Premature. Better is 2 Rb1 to prepare b3. **Rae8.** An ideal move. It develops an idle piece with gain of time—nothing more could be asked. 3 **Qd1?** Back to Hackensack! Instead of losing time more logical is 1 Nc3. **Re7 4 Nc3 Rfe8 5 Bd2 h5 6 Re1.** It's always a good idea to challenge an open file before the opponent's control of it becomes too dominating. **Rxe1+ 7 Bxe1 Nd4.** Threatening to invade on the light squares with ...Bg4. **8 Ne4 Qf5.** Black's pieces are beautifully posted and White's position is extremely difficult.

THE WRONG ROOK

EVANS—COLLINS

New Jersey 1950

Diagram 118

White moves. When rooks are connected and one of them can move to the center, annotators are in the sarcastic habit of writing "the wrong rook!" no matter which one goes there. White has a choice of 1 Rfd1 or Rad1 in order to bolster the pawn on d4 and later expand with e4. Black's two bishops compensate somewhat for his cramp. The immediate question is which rook should go to d1, and why?

1 Rfd1. The right rook! White chooses this because the other one belongs on c1. Before making a choice it's important to visualize where each rook will do the most good. **Rac8 2 Rac1 Qb8.** Black can do little but sit back and wait. His position is cramped but solid. **3 e4 b6 4 e5.** Something's gotta give! White can't maintain the central tension forever

and decides to invade on d6. **Nd5 5 Ne4 Rc7 6 Ned6.** Or
6 Ncd6 f5! 7 Nxe8 Rxe8=. If now 6...b5 7 Nxe8 Rxe8 8 Ne3
(to dislodge Black's only well-placed piece) Rec8 9 Be4 h6 10
Qb3 White has an edge in Space but Black's position is still a
tough nut to crack.

SITTING ON A POSITION

EVANS—HEATH

Texas 1949

Diagram 119

White moves. Nowhere is patience more a virtue than in
chess. A common fallacy is that every move should contain a
threat, but it's not always necessary to do something energetic.
In the absence of anything tactical, you should use the lull to
develop pieces or, if they are already developed, to find even
better squares for them. According to an old checker maxim,
"He who disturbs his position the least, disturbs his opponent
the most,"
    1 Rad1. This sits on the position by exerting masked
pressure on the d-file. It also brings a rook to the center and
discourages the freeing maneuver ...d5. The first question
White must ask himself is "where do I want my rooks?" If he

played 1 Rfd1 where would his put his a-rook later? **c5.** On 1...d5 2 Rfe1 increases the pressure. **2 Qxd7 Nxd7 3 Bxe7 Rxe7 4 f3.** White has an edge in Space and good chances to exploit the doubled pawns, but Black should be able to hold this endgame.

MAKING "LUFT"

HEARST—EVANS

New York 1947

Diagram 120

Black moves. Making *Luft* (the German word for air) is a way to create breathing space for the King on the back rank that can come in very handy. This garden variety position looks drawish, yet the skirmish is far from over. Before proceeding any further, both sides correctly use the lull to make *luft*.

1...h6 2 h3. Neither side now has to worry about an impromptu mate on the back rank. White has a queenside majority (3 pawns vs. 2). The king and pawn ending arising from this position is a theoretical draw, but just for fun. Remove all the pieces from the board and play it out with a friend (see Diagram 156(p. 179)).

GUARD THE BACK RANK

EVANS—COLLINS_____

New York 1947

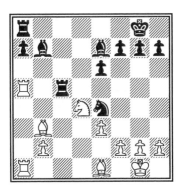

Diagram 121

White moves. Failing to make *luft* can have disastrous consequences. Correct is 1 h3 or even better 1 f3! gaining Time by attacking the knight and making *luft* for the king on f2. Instead watch what happened!

1 Rxa7?! Risky but not fatal. The best winning try is 1 R5a2 but for all practical purposes the safest way to safeguard the back rank is 1 f3 Rxa5 2 Rxa5 Nc5 3 Bc2 with equal chances. **Rxa7 2 Rxa7 Rc1 3 Nc2?** The losing move. White can still draw by 3 Kf1! Bb4 4 Nc2 Bxe1 5 Nxe1 Nc5 6 f3 (not 6 Bc2? Ba6+) Rb1 7 Bc2 Rxb2. **Nc5 4 f3 Bd6 5 Kf1 Ba6+ 6 Kg1 h6!** There's no rush and Black simply guards his back rank. White now gave up the Exchange and resigned shortly after **7 Rxa6 Nxa6..**

ESCAPE SQUARES

EVANS—PHILLIPS

New York 1949

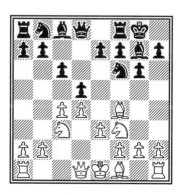

Diagram 122

White moves. An escape square is an alternate expression for *luft* when making a haven for a piece other than the king. How can White insure that his bishop on f4 remains on its excellent diagonal by creating an escape square for it?

1 h3. Such a move should only be played with good reason, especially when it involves a loss of Time before development has been completed. Since this is a relatively closed position, however, Time is relatively negligible and it was played on the supposition that sooner or later White will have to create an escape square for the bishop on h2 to guard against ...Nh5. Another point is that it restrains the bishop on c8 by taking g4 away from it. White has other good alternatives such as 1 Rc1 or Qb3. He can delay 1 Bd3 dxc4 2 Bxc4 which costs a tempo by moving the bishop twice.

Diagram 122 arises from a standard line in the Gruenfeld Defense: **1 d4 Nf6 2 c4 g6 3 Nc3 d5 4 Bf4 Bg7 5 e3 0–0 6 Nf3** (White snatched a dubious pawn in Evans—Gligoric, Amsterdam 1964 which was drawn in 44 moves after 6 cxd5

Nxd5 7 Nxd5 Qxd5 8 Bxc7 Na6 9 Bxa6 Qxg2 10 Qf3 Qxf3 11 Nxf3 bxa6 12 0-0 Bb7 13 Ne5 Rac8) **c6.**

OVERPROTECTION

NASH—EVANS

U.S. Open 1950

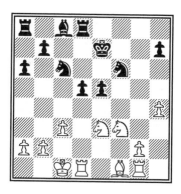

Diagram 123

Black moves. His highly mobile center pawns exert a cramping influence on White's awkwardly placed pieces, but which pawn should advance and when? 1...d4 looks reasonable, but surely not 1...e4? 2 Nd4 saddling Black with a backward d-pawn.

1...Be6. Black decides to delay the decision by developing a piece and keeping White guessing about which pawn will advance. This move also "overprotects" the pawn on d5 because, strictly speaking, Black has more pieces already defending it than are actually necessary for its safety. The game continued **2 Ng5 Bc8.** Temporizing. Also playable is 2...Bg8 3 Nf5+ Kf8. **3 g4?** Better is 3 Nf3 waiting to see if Black will acquiesce to a draw by repetition after 3...Be6 4 Ng5 Bc8 or finally decide on 3...d4! to take the initiative. **d4 4 cxd4 Nxd4 5 Kb1 h6 6 Nh3 Nf3 7 Rxd8 Kxd8 8 Rg3 Nd2+ 9 Kc1 Nxf1 10 Nxf1 Nxg4**

winning a pawn. Note how Black converted his liquidity in the center into material gain (Force).

OVERPROTECT WEAK POINTS

EVANS—NIELSEN_____

Olympics 1950

Diagram 124

White moves. Nimzovich's concept of overprotection dealt mainly with central pawns, but we may extend it to weak points anywhere on the board. White clearly has light square weaknesses on f3 and h3 which he fortifies with the temporizing **1 Kg2.** In such a complicated position, this move looks quite innocuous, but it actually came in handy later.

1 Kg2. Adhering to the first oath in medicine: Do no harm. White has an edge in Space but Black's position is fundamentally sound. **Nc5 2 Qb1 e6.** It's harder for White to make headway against 2...Ncd7 or even h6. **3 Bg5 Re8 4 Bd2 Ncd7 5 dxe6 Rxe6?** A costly error. Better is 5...fxe6. **6 Nd5! Rxc1 7 Qxc1 Qxa2 8 Nxb6 Rc6.** Forced. If 9...Nxb6 10 Rd8+ wins outright. **9 Rxd7! Rxc1 10 Rd8+ Bf8 11 Bxc1.** Gilding the lily. Quicker is 11 Bh6 Qa3 12 Nd7. **Kg7 12 Nd7 Qd5**

13 Bg5 Bb5 14 Rg8+ 1-0. On 14...Kxg8 15 Nf6+ forks the queen.

PAWNS ARE BATTERING RAMS

EVANS & SPIELBERGER—LOKVENCZ & PRAVDA
Consultation, Vienna 1956.

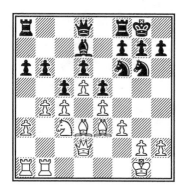

Diagram 125

White moves. Black's queenside looks pretty solid. White must use his pawns over there as battering rams to find a point of invasion. It's amazing how quickly he obtains undisputed control of the b-file and, with it, the vital b6 square with a base from which to strike at Black's backward pawn on d6.

1 a4 a5. To prevent a5 Black weakens b5. Equally bad was 1...axb4 2 Rxb4 Rb8 3 Rab1 piling up on b6. **2 bxc5 bxc5 3 Rb2 Rb8 4 Rxb8 Qxb8 5 Rb1 Qc7 6 Qb2!** White's advantage in Space is decisive because Black's can't challenge the only open file with Rb8. **Rc8 7 Qb6 Kf8 8 Qxc7 Rxc7 9 Rb6.** Invading this square is crucial and the rook can't be stopped from its foraging mission. **Ke7 10 Ra6 Rb7 11 Nb5 Ne8 12 Nxd6! Rb3.** If 12...Nxd6 13 Bxc5 wins easily. **13 Bxc5 Rxd3 14 Nb7+ 1-0.**

SECURE ADVANCED OUTPOSTS

EVANS (USA)–QUESADA (CUBA)_____

Radio match 1947

Diagram 126

White moves. He wants to secure f4 for his knight, an excellent post indeed. The fact that Black's king is still in the center permits him to do it with **1 h4!** Ordinarily this could be met by 1...h6 maintaining the pawn on g5, yet here after 2 hxg5 the pin is fatal because White's can't recapture. All this trouble because Black failed to connect his rooks!

1 h4! gxh4. Slightly better is 1...g4 which, it is true, weakens the dark squares. But the text makes an even greater concession by opening the h-file for White. **2 Rxh4 0-0-0 3 Nf4.** The knight has secured this post and can't be dislodged. White won shortly.

OCCUPY ADVANCED OUTPOSTS

EVANS—CARLYLE

U.S. Open 1952.

Diagram 127

White moves. Black is a pawn down but has some pressure as compensation. His immediate threat is ...Re8. White's knight is passive and burdened with protecting the d-pawn, yet there is a ray of light. How can White redeploy his knight so that it can reach a radiant paradise on e5?

1 Ng1! The horse beats a strategic retreat and is headed for f3 and e5. **Re8.** One move too late! **2 Nf3 Re7 3 Rxe7 Qxe7 4 Ne5.** White can now go to sleep—his game plays itself. The remaining moves were: **Qc7 5 Rc1 a6 6 h4 Qa7 7 Rd1 Qb7 8 Kh2 Qa7 9 Qc2.** With the double threat of Qxf5 and/or Bxd5. **Bxd4 10 Qxf5 Rb8 11 Nc6 1-0.**

TIME

Time is so precious that if a player with only mediocre ability were granted the right to move twice in a row just once each game he could become world champion.

Time is the unit of the move, the realm of tactics and tempi. In an ideal opening the king castles early and pieces are cleared rapidly from the back rank, allowing both rooks freely to shuttle towards open files. Battles are won, as in war, by the army that gets to the battlefield "fustest with the mostest." Pieces shackled in a cramped position can't reach the front line fast enough to be of help. Speed is essential. That's why beginners are admonished not to lose time in the opening by moving the same piece twice.

The "initiative" is an advantage in Time. The first move confers this driving force on White, but it's likely to dissipate unless pursued with vigor. After **1 e4** White threatens to dominate the center with **2 d4**. Like it or not, Black already is thrown on the defensive. The symmetrical **1...e5** has been the most popular reply for centuries. White can still play **2 d4**—but only at a cost. After **2...exd4 3 Qxd4** this early queen sortie is dubious because Black gains a tempo with **3...Nc6** compelling the queen to move again, thus delaying the development of a minor piece (bishop or knight).

Diagram 128

Black gains a tempo. White must move his queen once more, preferably to a4. But a tempo is lost whenever the same piece must move twice. If White balks at recapturing the pawn with his queen after **1 e4 e5 2 d4 exd4** he may elect the risky gambit **3 c3!?** which can be met in a number of ways.

GAMBITS

A gambit is an attempt to forcibly seize the initiative by sacrificing material. The gambiteer hopes to profit from his rapid development and superior mobility to score an early knockout, or to regain his investment with interest. But it stands to reason the second player has little to fear if has made no errors and incurred no organic weaknesses, When a pawn sacrifice doesn't pay off quickly, the attacker faces almost certain defeat against accurate defense. *"If I don't commit an error I fancy that I shall win because I have a pawn to the good and according to the principles I laid down, I must win,"* is how Steinitz put the matter.

But thanks to their shock value gambits can still pack a wallop. The Evans Gambit **1 e4 e5 2 Nf3 Nf6 3 Bc4 Bc5 4 b4!?** has a terrific track record in the tournament arena and fares better than most conventional openings. One database containing 519 games from 1826 to 2006 with this ploy reveals that White won 51.1%, Black won 34.1%, with only 14.8% drawn! Kasparov, during his reign as world champion, successfully revived the Evans Gambit in 1995 against future titleholder Anand.

The word for gambit is derived from "gambetta," Italian for tripping up a rival's legs in wrestling. There are three ways to respond: **(1)** To decline. **(2)** To hold doggedly onto the sacrificed material and surrender the initiative. **(3)** To accept and then return material at a favorable moment. Let's examine the Danish Gambit after **1 e4 e5 2 d4 exd4 3 c3!?**

1st method—Declining the gambit with **3...d5.** Weaker is 3...d3 because White retrieves his material with 4 Bxd3 and also brings out a fresh piece.

GAMBIT DECLINED

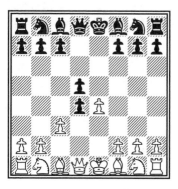

Diagram 129
Position after 3...d5

Black opens lines and fights White in his own element—Time against Time! A possible continuation is **4 exd5 Qxd5 5 cxd4 Nc6 6 Nf3 Bg4 7 Be2 0-0-0** (not 7...Bxf3? 8 Bxf3

Qxd4? 9 Bxc6+ bxc6 10 Qxd4) **8 Nc3 Qa5** with superior development and lasting pressure against the isolated d-pawn.

2nd method—Holding doggedly onto the sacrificed material, hoping to weather the storm. **1 e4 e5 2 d4 exd4 3 c3 dxc3 4 Bc4?!** White sticks to the true spirit of a gambit by not stopping for 4 Nxc3, aiming instead for quick development at all cost. **4...cxb2 5 Bxb2 c6.**

GAMBIT ACCEPTED

Diagram 130
Position after 5...c6

Black willingly submits to an attack in the firm resolve that White lacks sufficient compensation for two sacrificed pawns. Thus Black is fighting White in another element— Force against Time! Now the question is whether Black can withstand the fury of the attack and emerge into the beatific endgame which his material superiority promises.

Notice that Black hasn't developed a single piece, whereas White has two bishops bearing down on menacing diagonals, yet Black is prepared to suffer because he has no organic weaknesses in his Pawn Structure. A possible continuation is **6 Nc3 d6 7 Nf3 Nd7 8 0-0 Ngf6.** If White can't quickly exploit his initiative, Black will nullify it and catch up in development.

Black has a big plus but a final evaluation depends on your style: An attacker likes White; a defender likes Black. Choose your poison!

3rd method—Accepting and then returning the pawn at a favorable moment: **1 e4 e5 2 d4 exd4 3 c3 dxc3 4 Bc4 cxb2 5 Bxb2 d5.**

GAMBIT ACCEPTED—AND RETURNED

Diagram 131
Position after 5...d5

The principle behind 5...d5 is so potent that gambits have all but vanished from modern tournaments! Black fights back in yet another element—Pawn Structure against Time! By returning material to blunt the attack, Black hopes to simplify and swap queens to reach a favorable endgame.

A possible continuation is **6 Bxd5.** 6 exd5 closes the diagonal and leaves Black a pawn up with an easy defense after 6...Nf6 7 Nf3 Bd6 8 0-0 0-0 9 Nc3 Bg4 10 Qd4 Nbd7 as in Opocensky-Reti, Baden 1914. Once Black gets his king out of the center, he's safe. **Nf6! 7 Bxf7+ Kxf7 8 Qxd8 Bb4+** The temporary sacrifice of the queen is a good example of a strategical theme bolstered by tactical execution. **9 Qd2 Bxd2+ 10 Bxd2 Re8.**

Black made no attempt to refute the gambit but is content with a slight pull in an endgame likely to be drawn in view of the opposite colored bishops. But if this is the best White can get, then obviously he will abandon the Danish Gambit, and that's exactly what has happened at the master level. This antidote put many gambits out of business. The principle of accepting and then returning material in a timely fashion frustrates the psychology of the attacker by throwing him on the defensive when he is in an aggressive frame of mind.

CONCEPTS IN TIME

USELESS CHECKS

EVANS—FLORES

New York 1947

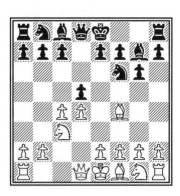

Diagram 132

White moves. The Gruenfeld Defense: **1 d4 Nf6 2 c4 g6 3 Nc3 Bg7 4 Bf4 0-0.** Many moves have been tried here for White without yielding a clear-cut advantage. A check is a loss of time if it helps the defender improve his position, but to take my opponent out of the book I tested **5 Qa4+!?** even though "Always check, it may be mate" is a glittering epigram that belongs in the trash heap. **Bd7!** Best. There are several ways to go wrong. If 5...c6? 6 Bxb8! Rxb8 7 Qxa7 Bf5 8 c5 wrests a pawn. Or 5...Nc6? 6 Nb5! **6 Qb3 Nc6.** Stronger than 6...Bc6 7 e4! e6 8 cxd5 exd5 8 Be5! **7 e3.** You can't neglect development forever. Too risky is 7 Qxb7? Nxd4 8 0-0-0 Ne6. **Na5 8 Qb4 Nxc4 9 Bxc4 dxc4 10 Qxb7 Rb8?** Finally going wrong. On 10...Qb8! 11 Qxb8+ Rxb8 12 0-0-0 Rb7 at best the chances are equal because Black's two bishops outweigh his inferior Pawn Structure. **11 Qxa7 Rxb2 12 Nf3 Bc6.** Black has the initiative but it's not enough to compensate for his lost material and White prevailed after **13 Bxc7 Qc8 14 Bg3 0-0 15 0-0 Bxf3 16 gxf3.**

Checking merely for the sake of checking is a good way of working out spite but often backfires. If White knew that **5 Qa4+** was dubious, one is tempted to wonder why he did it. The answer lies in the ever-constant search for innovations. Each position is as distinct as a fingerprint and modern masters spend a lot of spare time searching for refinements. Even when a move is inferior, it can still pack a punch that catches an opponent off guard.

WASTED MOVES

ASH—EVANS

New York 1946

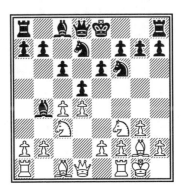

Diagram 133

Black moves. We generally think of a move as wasted when it has no particular plan or costs a tempo we can't afford to lose. Sometimes it simply reflects excessive caution, as I learned in my very first tournament game in the Marshall Club Junior Championship.

1...h6? A wasted move if ever there was one. To begin with, it neglects castling, contributes nothing towards development, and ignores the task of freeing the bishop on c8. Moreover, this move has no bearing on the action taking place in the center. Much better is **1...dxc4** making it hard if not impossible for White to regain the pawn. Even **1...0-0** makes much more sense. The only justification for **1...h6** is that it prevents Bg5. But why go to the trouble of preventing it? Once the bishop gets to g5, then ...h6 breaks the pin by putting the question to the bishop.

POINTLESS THREATS
MEET THE SCHOLAR'S MATE_____

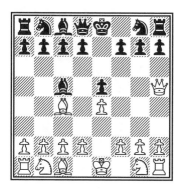

Diagram 134
Position after 3 Qh5

Black moves. Another common failing of the beginner is to lay a trap and then bite his nails hoping the other guy will overlook it. This is shabby chess. Even if it works for you, which it probably did a few times in the past, it only speaks poorly for the victim. If you really want to improve, always assume your opponent will find the best reply and plan your next move accordingly. Play the board, not the player!

Don't hatch traps that are likely to explode in your face. This position arose after **1 e4 e5 2 Bc4 Bc5 3 Qh5!?** White threatens mate-in-one—The Scholar's Mate—which can be easily foiled with proper defense. **Qe7!** Guarding e5 as well as f7 while leaving f6 free for the knight. **4 Nf3 Nc6 5 0-0.** If 5 Ng5? Bxf2+! 5 Kxf2 Qc5+ 6 Ke1 Qxc4 7 Na3 Nf6! repulses the attack. **Nf6.** Black gains a tempo by harrying the misplaced queen and stands slightly better after **6 Qh4 d6.**

Moral: Don't bring out the queen too soon.

PREMATURE ATTACKS

STEINER—EVANS

6th match game 1952

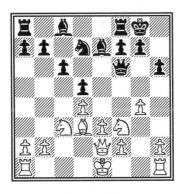

Diagram 135

Black moves. An attack is likely to boomerang unless adequate measures are taken to prevent a counterattack. Eager for an early knockout, known in boxing as "headhunting," White left his king in the center and launched an offensive with **1 g4?** The clever refutation is **1...Nc5! 2 Ne5.** Forced. If 2 dxc5 Bxg4 wins a pawn since White has no way to support his pinned knight on f3. And 2 Bb1 Bxg4 3 Qc2 g6 4 Ne5 Bf5 snags a pawn and thwarts the attack. **Nxd3+ 3 Nxd3 Qh4.** Black swapped a passive knight for an active bishop and seized the initiative.

Moral: Complete development first—attack later.

USEFUL CHECKS

MECHANIC—EVANS

Diagram 136

Black moves. It's obvious Black must move his bishop before he can castle. But where? 1...Be7 is fine but more forceful is **1...Bb4+!** Gains a tempo by forcing White to retreat, whereupon Black can castle—two moves for the price of one! **2 Ned2 0-0 3 a3 Be7.** White has a slight spatial advantage while Black still must solve the problem of freeing his "problem child" on c8, probably to b7 after ...b6 and c5.

PLAY IT SAFE
WHAT SHOULD BLACK DO? _____

Diagram 137

Black moves. He is already two pawns ahead with a bewildering array of tempting defenses at his disposal. **1...dxc3** or **Nxc3** or **Nd6** all look good—but which one is best? Solving this dilemma in a tournament game with the clock ticking could cost the game if you run short of time—even if you find the best move. Since Black already has enough material to win, why be greedy? Forget about finding the very best move and concentrate on making safe passage for the king by castling with all due speed.

As a practical matter the simplest solution is **1...Nxc3 2 bxc3 Be7 3 cxd4 d5 4 Bd3 0-0.** Black gave back booty but his king is safe and he is still a pawn ahead in a winning position. Other moves may be even better, but why endure an arduous defense by grabbing more material? Some discredited Soviet analysis claims that White gets a fierce attack after **1...dxc3 2 Bxf7+?! Kxf7 3 Qd5+ Ke8 4 Re1 Be7 5 Rxe4 d6 6 Bg5** but this is refuted by **Kf8 7 Bxe7+ Nxe7 8 Rf4+ Nf5 9 Rxf5+ Bxf5 10 Qxf5+ Qf6.** Also sufficient is **1... Nd6** which leads to tricky complications after **2 Nd5?! Nxc4**

3 Bg5. But why bother trying to sort out this mess over-the-board when a simple defense wins? Although **1...Nxc3** may not be theoretically best, it's the right way to go if you land in uncharted territory.

Moral: Safety first! When confronted with several attractive alternatives seek the simplest one, even though it's not best, if it avoids trouble.

AGGRESSIVE DEFENSE

MCCORMICK—EVANS

Diagram 138

Black moves. He is two pawns ahead but not exactly happy in view of two major threats: 1 Bd4 or 1 Qxf5! gxf5 2 Rxh6 mate. Passivity be damned! Black must seek an aggressive defense before it's too late—even though, as neither side was aware of at the time, it's already too late!

1...Qe2! The only good defense throws White off balance. **2 Qxf5?** The sockdolager is hard to find with the clock ticking: 2 Rxg6! (if 2 Bd4 Qf3+ 3 Kh3 Qg4+ 4 Kg2 draws) Kxg6 3 Qe6+ Kh5 (not 4 Kh7? Qxh6 mate) 4 h3! Qd1+ 5 Kh2 does the trick. **Qxe3! 3 Qxg6+ Kh8 4 Rf6 Rxf2+! 5 Rxf2 Qxf2+ 7 Kxf2 Bd4+ 7 Ke2 Rxg6 0-1.**

COUNTERATTACK

EVANS—HARTLEB

U.S. Open 1948

Diagram 139

White moves. Passive positions limit mobility and should be shunned whenever possible. White's dilemma is where to move his knight which either can retreat to d1 (passive) or advance to d5 (swapping) or capture a pawn (Nxb5) but none of these choices seems to inspire confidence.

1 e5!? Ignoring the knight in order to counterattack, touching off a combination based on the momentary alignment of Black's queen and rook on the h2-b8 diagonal. In retrospect 1 Nd5! Nxd5 2 exd5 Bd6 3 Qd3 was the right decision, but certainly not 1 Nxb5? Rxb5 2 Qxb5 Qxc2 gathering two pieces for the rook. **dxc3 2 exf6 Bxf6 3 Qe4 g6 4 Bf4 Qc5?** Correct is 4...Qb6! 5 Bxb8 cxb2 6 Rad1 Bf5 7 Qe2 Bxc2 8 Qxc2 Rxb8 with advantage. **5 b4! Qb6 6 Bxb8 Bf5 7 Qf4 Qxb8 8 Qxb8 Rxb8 9 Bxf5 gxf5 10 Ra6 Bg5 11 Rc6 Bd2 12 Re5.** White won this ending which has now devolved into a matter of technique.

SUSTAIN THE INITIATIVE

EVANS—FLORIDO

U.S. Open 1953

Diagram 140

White moves. Black hopes to challenge White's grip on the d-file with ...Rd8. What White must do is weaken the base of Black's queenside pawns by making new threats. Note that 1 Rd7 Rc7 doesn't solve the problem.

1 Nb5! a6. Black has no time for Rd8 and must advance this pawn, thus weakening his b-pawn. If 1...Ra8 2 Rd7 a6 3 Nd6 penetrates decisively. **2 Nc3.** The deed is done. Time was converted into Pawn Structure and Black must lose a pawn because his pawn chain is undermined. **Rd8.** Striving for counterplay. If 3...Rb8 4 Nd5 wins. **3 Rxd8+.** Also good is 3 Rxb6 but White prefers to simplify before gaining a pawn. **Nxd8 4 Nd5 b5 5 Nc7 Ne6 7 Nxa6 c4 8 Ke3.** The rest, to coin a phrase, is a matter of technique.

INTERPOLATIONS

BRONSTEIN (USSR)—EVANS (USA)

Team match, Moscow 1955

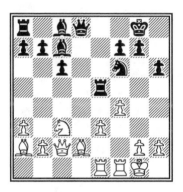

Diagram 141

Black moves. An interpolation is an in-between move (see Diagrams 12 and 13 (p. 35) for classic examples). Black's rook is attacked and must retreat, but not without a little finesse. After 1...Re8 which is perfectly good he must worry about White's expansion in the center with e4 sooner or later.

1...Bf5! 2 e4. Now or never, even if it costs a pawn. After 2 Qc1 (or Qb3) Re7 Black cements his grip on the center. Bronstein doesn't want to be stuck with a backward e-pawn and a hole on e4. **Bb6+ 3 Kh1 Rxe4! 4 Nxe4 Nxe4 5 Nxe4 Bxe4 6 Qxe4 Qxd2 7 Bb1 Rd8.** Black is a pawn up but it's not enough to win after 8 Qh7+ Kf8 9 Qh8+ Ke7 10 Qxg7 Qxf4! 11 Re1+ (not 11 Rxf4?? Rd1+ mates) Kd7 12 Ba2. **7 Bc2? Kf8 8 Re1 Bc5 9 h3 g6 10 Rd1 Qa5.** After some inaccuracies in time-pressure the game ended in a draw due to opposite colored bishops.

ZWISCHENZUG

KRAMER—EVANS

New York 1952

Diagram 142

Black moves. *Zwischenzug* is a German endearment reserved for aesthetic examples of interpolation such as this. Black is a piece up and 1...Qxc6 2 bxc3 Qxc3 wins a pawn, although White gets some open lines as compensation. It looks like Black has to enter this variation. After all, his queen is attacked twice and must skedaddle—must it not?

1...Nd4!? A *zwischenzug* in its full glory! Black ignores the obvious threat to his queen and blithely proceeds to counterattack. **2 Qe3?** Dazed and confused, the queen finds the wrong haven. Better is 2 Qd3! Qg4 3 Bd6! Bxb2 4 cxb7 Bxa1 5 bxa8/Q Rxa8 6 Rxa1 Rd8 7 h3=. **Qxc6 3 bxc3 Nc2 4 Qg3 Nxa1 5 Rxa1 Rfe8.** Black has won the Exchange and the rest is easy.

CONVERT TIME INTO PAWN STRUCTURE

MAYER—EVANS

U.S. Junior Championship 1949

Diagram 143

Black moves. For the nonce he is a piece down but there is no rush to recapture it with 1...Kxd7. Instead an interpolation allows him to convert the less durable advantage (Time) into a more durable one (Pawn Structure).

1...Bxc3+! Mission accomplished. 1...Kxd7 is okay but gives White a chance to prevent doubled pawns by 2 Bd2! Rfe8+ 3 Kf1 d4 4 Nb1—ugly but perhaps tenable. **2 bxc3 Kxd7 3 f3 c5 4 Be3 Kc6 5 Rb1 Nd7.** Headed for the hole on c4. 5...Rhe8 first is also good. **6 Kd2 Nb6 7 Rhe1 Rhe8 8 Bf2 Nc4+ 9 Kd3 Na3 10 Rxe8 Rxe8 11 Rb2.** Better is 11 Re1. **f5 12 Bg3?** Hastens the end. **Nc4 0-1.** There's no defense to the double threat of Re3 mate and/or Nxb2+.

CONVERT TIME INTO SPACE

Hollywood 1954

Diagram 144

Black moves. Timing is always crucial. If White's were on move, then 1 h3! would strengthen his fortress. Black wants to double rooks by Raa2 and invade on the 2nd rank but first must undermine the bishop on f3 which is guarding the pawn on g2.

1...Bg4! 2 Rf1? A tougher defense gives drawing chances after 2 h4 Bxf3 3 gxf3 Raa2 4 Rb6+ Kg7 5 Rb5 Rg2+ 6 Kh1 Rh2+ 7 Kg1 Rag2+ 8 Kf1 Rb2 9 Kg1 Rhg2+ 10 Kh1 Rgf2 11 Rxe5 Rxf3 12 Rxh5 Rxb4. **Raa2 3 h4 Bxf3 4 Rxf3 Rxg2+ 5 Kf1 Rgb2 6 Kg1 Rb1+ 7 Rf1 Rxf1+ 8 Kxf1 Rh2 9 Rb5 f6 10 Rc5 Rxh4 11 Rc4 Rh2 12 Ke1 h4 13 Kd1 h3 14 Rc3 Kg5 15 Rb3 Kg4 0-1.** It's curtains after 16 b5 Ra2 17 b6 h2.

PINS

THE PIN IS MIGHTIER THAN THE SWORD

MCCORMICK—EVANS_____

New York 1947

Dagram 145

Black moves. A pin is a combination Space-Time advantage. Time in the sense that the pinned piece is momentarily tied down. Space in the sense that the pinned piece dare not advance. The pawn on c4 can't move without exposing the queen behind it to capture. How can this be exploited?

1...b5! 2 Nd5. Nothing can avert the loss of at least a pawn. If 2 Nxb5 a6 wins a piece based upon yet another infernal pin, and White doesn't get enough compensation for it after 3 a4 axb5 4 axb5 d5. **bxc4 3 Nxe7+ Nxe7.** Black has won a pawn with a crushing position, but somehow White got too much counterplay and later missed a win. (See Diagram 138 (p. 163) for the finale).

SOME PINS ARE FOREVER

LEVIN—EVANS

U.S. Open 1946

Diagram 146

Black moves. The beauty of a pin is that sometimes there's no rush to release it because the pinned piece can't run away. White is a pawn down with some pressure, yet a single blow by Black shatters his game. **1...Nxc4! 2 Rxc4 d6!** What's the hurry? Black is hunting for bigger game than 2...Bxc4 3 Qxc4. There's no rush to capture the rook until White moves his queen to break the pin. **3 Bc3 Rxe1+ 4 Bxe1 Re8.** Another hammer blow. **5 Bc3 Bxc4.** The time is ripe to cash in. **6 Qxc4 Re4 7 Qc6 Rxf4.**

Moral: Squeeze the last drop out of a pin—there's no rush to release it. Patience is a virtue.

HIDDEN PINS

KRAUSS—EVANS

U.S. Junior Championship 1949

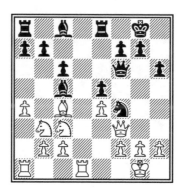

Diagram 147

Black moves. Not all pins are obvious. In fact, here it's hard to tell just which of White's pieces is pinned—even potentially! Black's bishop is under fire and must retreat, must it not?

1...Nh3+! The g-pawn is wedded to the queen and can't capture this upstart. **2 Kf1 Qxf3 3 gxf3 Bxf2 4 Bd2 Bh4.** White is a pawn behind and his Pawn Structure is shattered. I trust that anyone who got this far in the book has acquired enough technique to win this endgame.

PUTTING THE QUESTION TO THE BISHOP
THE RUY LOPEZ

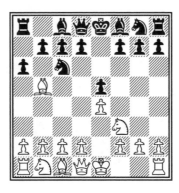

Diagram 148
Position after 3...a6

White moves. This is the famed Morphy Defense: **1 e4 e5 2 Nf3 Nc6 3 Bb5 a6**. The last move "puts the question to the bishop," a genial phrase originating with Nimzovich who preached that pins—even potential ones —should be broken as soon as possible. What's the purpose of **3...a6** which looks so innocuous? In effect, it forces the bishop either to retreat or swap for the knight —- but either way White must declare his intentions! "Putting the question" makes the bishop choose between occupying the f1-a6 diagonal or the a4-e8 diagonal. See Diagram 16 (p. 41) for **4 Bxc6 dxc6 5 d4**. Much weaker is 5 Nxe5? Qd4 regaining the pawn advantageously. **exd4 6 Qxd4 Qxd4 7 Nxd4.**

The point of **3...a6** is to ease the pressure against the pawn on e5. After **4 Ba4** (the most popular reply) Black doesn't have to chase it again with 4...b5 but can calmly pursue development with **Nf6**. The fact that the bishop is on a4 instead of b5 means the pin now can be broken in only one move (b5) instead of

two (a6 and b5) which can come in handy. E.g., **5 0-0 Be7
6 d4?! exd4 7 Nxd4? Nxd4 8 Qxd4 c5 9 Q-any c4** snares
the bishop (Noah's Ark Trap). Of course this trap is not the
justification of **3...a6** which is just a useful interpolation with
nothing to lose and much to gain.

MASKED ATTACKS

EVANS—JIMENEZ

Cuba 1952

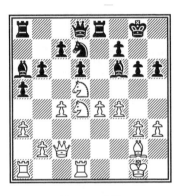

Diagram 149

White moves. A masked attack is a kind of hidden pin.
There are two meaningful ones here: (1) The rook on d1 exerts
a masked attack against the queen despite the fact that four
men intervene. (2) The bishop on g2 exerts a masked attack
against the rook on a8 despite the intervention of two men.
White's task is to open both lines and gain material.

1. e5! dxe5. The offer of a pawn neither can be accepted
nor rejected! If 1...Bg7 2 Nc6 Qc8 3 Nde7+ Rxe7 4 Nxe7+ forks
the queen. **2 Nc6.** Occupying the hole! **Qc8 3 fxe5 Bd8.** No
help is 3...Bg5 4 h4 Bb7 5 hxg5 Bxc6 6 Bh3 Bxd5 7 Rxd5 Re7
8 Rad1 piling on the pin. **4 Nxd8 Rxd8.** Equally futile is 4...
Qxd8 5 Nf6+. **5 Ne7+ 1-0.**

QUIZ!

A WORD OF CAUTION

This unique quiz features thirty-six snapshots plucked from my tournament games. You not only are asked to find the right move but also to identify the principle used to arrive at this decision. The solutions refer you back to the diagrams where these principles are discussed.

It's often been said that strategy is what to do when there is nothing to do, while tactics is what to do when there is something to do. So far we have spoken of abstractions such as Pawn Structure, Space, Force and Time. These elements often overlap, and now the time has come for you to assemble all the pieces of the jigsaw and meld strategy and tactics in order to play a creditable game.

Chess is an art form and there is room for dissent. The answers reflect my own reasoning, so don't be surprised if your computer doesn't always agree with me. The only thing "new" about my system is how it's formulated.

PROBLEMS

DIAGRAM 150 _____

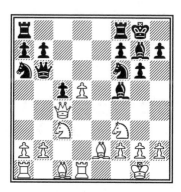

What should White do? What principles are involved?

DIAGRAM 151 _____

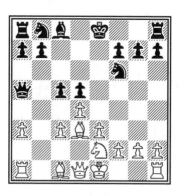

What should Black do? On what principle?

DIAGRAM 152_____

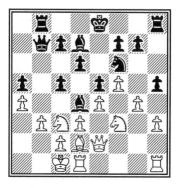

What should Black do? On what principle?

DIAGRAM 153_____

Where are White's holes? What should Black do?
On what principle?

DIAGRAM 154

What should Black do? On what principle?

DIAGRAM 155

What should Black do? On what principle?

DIAGRAM 156

Who has the outside passed pawn?
Black to move—what result?

DIAGRAM 157

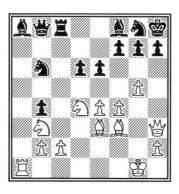

What should White do?

DIAGRAM 158

Where is the base of Black's pawn on d5?
Whose pawn structure is better?

DIAGRAM 159

Should Black play 1...d5 or d6?

DIAGRAM 160

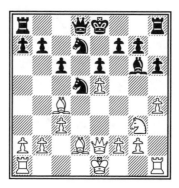

Where is White's hole? How can Black exploit it?

DIAGRAM 161

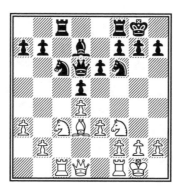

Who has the good bishop and why?

DIAGRAM 162

Where is Black's hole? How can White exploit it?

DIAGRAM 163

How can Black win a pawn? On what principle?

DIAGRAM 164

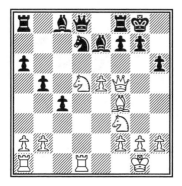

How can White convert his Space advantage into Force?

DIAGRAM 165

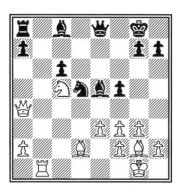

How can White win a piece? On what principle?

DIAGRAM 166

How can Black exploit the weak squares to win a piece?

DIAGRAM 167

Why is 1 Qxd4 bad?

DIAGRAM 168

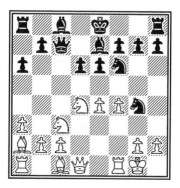

How can Black win material?

DIAGRAM 169

On which color squares is White weak?
What should Black do?

DIAGRAM 170

What should White do? On what principle?

DIAGRAM 171

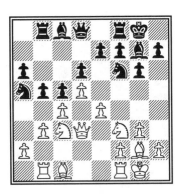

How can Black win a pawn?

DIAGRAM 172

Why is 1 e4 premature?

DIAGRAM 173

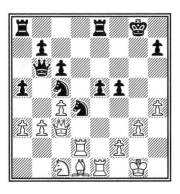

Should White play 1 Rxe5?

DIAGRAM 174

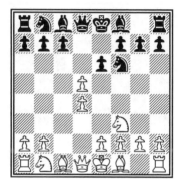

How should Black recapture the pawn? On what principle?

DIAGRAM 175

What should Black do? On what principle?

DIAGRAM 176_____

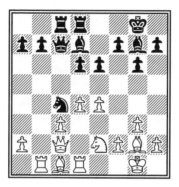

Who has the better game and why?

DIAGRAM 177_____

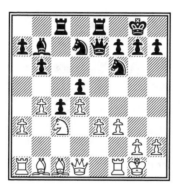

How can White mobilize his rook on a1?

DIAGRAM 178

How can White mobilize his center pawns?

DIAGRAM 179

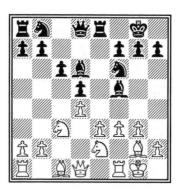

Is 1 e4 playable?

DIAGRAM 180

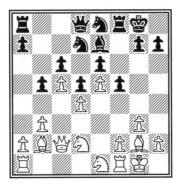

Black just played f5. Should White take en passant by 1 exf6?

DIAGRAM 181

Black just played b6. Why is it inferior?

DIAGRAM 182

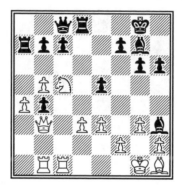

White has a strong interpolation. What is it?

DIAGRAM 183

Is 1 0-0 or Qc2 more accurate?

DIAGRAM 184

What should Black do and why?

DIAGRAM 185

Is a5 or e4 more accurate for Black?

SOLUTIONS

150. Evans—Heinkenheimo, Helsinki Olympiad 1952. (See Diagrams 108 (p. 130), 119 (p. 141), 120 (p. 142).) White has a comfortable spatial edge with well-posted pieces but there is nothing forceful at his disposal, so he uses the lull to stop for **1 h3** which makes *luft* and cuts off Black access to g5. The main principle involved is restriction. The alternative 1 Nh4 Bd7 strands the knight on a limb and accomplishes little. The same goes for 1 Na4 Qb4.

151. Evans—Sandrin, U.S. Open 1949, (See Diagram 42 (p.63).) Correct is **1...cxd4!** on the principle of forcing White to accept a backward c-pawn on an open file after 2 exd4 0-0. It's now or never! Inferior is 1...0-0 2 0-0 cxd4 (too late!) 3 cxd4! which straightens out the Pawn Structure.

152. Berliner—Evans, U.S. Junior Championship 1946. (See Diagram 66 (p. 84).) **1... c4!** on the principle of striking a pawn chain at its base. This move is tactically justified in view of 2 dxc4 Nxe4 (ot even 2...Bxa4 3 Nd2 Bc6).

153. Plater—Evans, Helsinki Olympiad 1952. (See Diagram 57 (p. 76).) White has holes on a3, d3, f3 and h3 and hopes to play d4. Black can hamper his development by occupying the hole with **1...Qd3!** White now struggled like a harpooned whale and incurred more light square weaknesses after 2 f4 Nc6 3 fxe5 Bg4 4 Bf3 Bxf3 5 Rxf3 Nxe5 6 Rf1 g5. This restraining move weakens the Pawn Structure but prevents Nf4 once and for all.

154. Pilnick—Evans, Marshall Club Championship 1949-50. (See Diagram 40 (p. 61).) **1...c5!** on the principle of repairing the isolated pawn on c6 and exerting pressure on the backward pawn at c3 (the immediate threat is c4).

155. Shaffer—Evans, U.S. Open 1949. (See Diagrams 44, 45, 46 (p.65-p.66).) Correct is **1...d5!** on the principle of repairing the backward d-pawn. With best play the game should be drawn after **2 cxd5 cxd5 3 Ncxd5 Nxd5 4 Nxd5 Nxd5**

5 Bxg7 Kxg7 6 exd5 Rxe1 7 Rxe1 Rxe1 8 Qc3+ Kg8 9 Qxe1 Qxd5.

156. Hearst—Evans, Marshall Club Junior Championship 1947. (See Diagram 15 (p. 40).) Black has the outside passed pawn but it's not enough to win after **1...g3 2 fxg3 fxg3 3 Kf3 Kc5 4 Kxg3 Kb4 5 Kf3 Ka3 6 Ke4 a5! Not 6...Kxa2?? 7 b4!** followed by c5 and White wins! **7 Kd3 Kxa2 8 Kc2 Draw.** It all hinges on a tempo. If Black's pawn were on a5 to begin with, he wins!

157. Jackson—Evans, Log Cabin Club Championship 1950. (See Diagrams 67 (p. 85), 68 (p. 86).) **1 g6! fxg6 2 Nxe6.** Black's Pawn Structure is a shambles now that its base has been disrupted.

158. Typical French Defense formation. (See diagrams 62, 63 (p. 81).) The base of Black's d-pawn is f7. White's d-pawn has no base and his light squares are weak. On balance Black's pawn chain is more solid and slightly better.

159. Kellner—Evans, U.S. Open 1950. (See Diagrams 18 (p. 43), 61 (p. 80).) Neither move is really better, it all depends on your style. **1...d6** is less committed and more flexible. Black can always push this pawn later, but it can never retreat. The game continued **2 h3 Nbd7 3 0-0 e5 4 e4 Nh5** with equal chances.

160. Hearst—Evans, Marshall Club Junior Championship 1946. (See Diagrams 54 (p. 73), 60 (p. 79)). There are several good ways to exploit White's hole on d3.
   (a) The stolid **1...N5b6 2 f4.** If 2 Bb3 Nc5 is crushing. **Nxc4 3 Qxc4 Nb6 4 Qe2 Qd5.** Black dominates.
   (b) The cunning **1...Qc7.** Forces White to weaken his light squares even more. **2 f4 b5 3 Bxd5 cxd5.**

(c) The forceful **1...b5 2 Bxd5 cxd5.** Now 3 Qxb5? Rb8 is in Black's favor, and 3 h5 Bh7 4 Qg4 Rg8 rebuffs the attack.

(d) The aggressive **1...Qa5 2 f4 0-0-0.**

(e) The tame **1...0-0** is also adequate.

161. Evans—Hans, match 1946. (See Diagram 69 (p. 88).) White has the good bishop which has greater mobility because most of his pawns are on dark squares. Black's bishop is momentarily hemmed in by its own pawns.

162. Hearst—Evans, U.S. Open 1953. (See Diagram 58 (p. 77).) Black's hole is on b6 and White exploited it to win a pawn by **1 Nc4! Qd8 2 Nxd5 Nxd5 3 Bxd5 exd5.** Worse is 3...Qxd5? 4 Nb6 Qxb3 5 axb3 Rb8 6 Bf4. **4 Nb6 Rb8 5 Nxc8 Rxc8 6 Rxc8 Qxc8 7 Qxd5.**

163. Evans—Harrold, Marshall Club Championship 1946-47. (See Diagram 137 (p. 162).) **1...Nxe4 2 Bxe7 Qxe7 3 Bxe4 Qb4+ 4 Qd2 Qxb2 5 0-0 Qa3.** Black snatches a pawn and lives to tell the tale. The principle is timely liquidation in order to convert Time into Force.

164. Evans—Rehberg, Marshall Club Championship 1949-50. (See Diagram 106 (p. 128).) **1 e6! fxe6 2 Qxe6+ Rf7 3 Nc7 Nf8.** No help is 3...Qf8 4 Rxd7 Bxd7 5 Qxd7 Rxf4 6 Nxa8. **4 Rxd8 Bxe6 5 Rxa8 Rxf4 6 Nxe6. 1-0.**

165. Evans—Bills, U.S. Open 1954. (See Diagram 125 (p. 147).) **1 f4! 1-0.** If 1...Bd6 2 Bxd5+ wins a piece because Black can't recapture without dropping his queen. The principles are pin and masked attack.

166. Dunst—Evans, Marshall Club Championship 1946-47. (See Diagram 54 (p. 73).) **1...Bf5! 2 Qe2.** The queen is overloaded, like an electric circuit. This loses a piece but there is no salvation anyway. If 2 Qd5 Rc5 3 Qa8+ Kg7 4 Qb7+ Rc7 5 Qd5 Rd8 6 Kh1 Be7 7 Rxe7+ Qxe7 8 Qxf5 Rxc4 9 Re1 Qf6. **Qd4+ 3 Kh1 Qxc4. 0-1.**

167. Evans—Lambert, Dubrovnik Olympiad 1950. (See Diagram 149 (p. 174).) 1 Qxd4? Nxe4! opens a masked attack, inviting 2 Qxe4? Re8 which pins the queen. The game continued: **1 Ne2 Re8 2 f3 c5 3 dxc6 bxc6 4 Nxd4 Qb6.** Black's strong counterplay on the dark squares regained the pawn and it ended in a lively draw. (As overall high scorer in my first international team tournament I won a gold medal with 8 wins in 10 games; this was one of my two draws).

168. Cross—Evans, U.S. Open 1955. (See Diagrams 54 (p. 73), 59 (p. 78).) Correct is **1...e5! 2 Nf3 Qc5+ 3 Kh1 Nf2+ 4 Rxf2 Qxf2** gaining the Exchange. Black won after 5 fxe5 dxe5 6 Nxe5 Be6.

169. Ulvestad—Evans, Hollywood 1954. (See Diagram 60 (p. 79).) White can't prevent a fatal penetration on his weak dark squares (a3, b2, c3, d4, e3, f4, g3, h4). The game continued **1...Na8!! 2 Qe2 Nb6 3 Nxb6 Qc3! 4 Nxd7 Kxd7 5 Ra2 Qxg3+ 7 Kf1 Rh8 0-1.**

170. Evans—LeCornu, U.S. Open 1952. (See Diagrams 59 (p. 78), 79 (p. 101).) Correct is **1 Ne5!** on the principle of using a pin to expose weak squares. White wants to undermine the backward pawn on e6 by getting rid of the bishop on f7. **Qe8.** If 1...fxe5 2 dxe5 Rd7 (the bishop on d6 is pinned) 3 exd6 Rxd6 4 f4 with an overwhelming spatial advantage. **2 Nxf7 Qxf7 3 f4 Kh8 4 Rd2** followed by Rde2 piling up on e6.

171. Kashdan—Evans, Hollywood 1954. (See Diagram 147 (p. 172).) There are two ways to win a pawn, but one is bad. The game continued: **1...b4!** Weaker is 1...bxc4 2 bxc4 Rxb1 3 Nxb1 Nxe4? 4 Qxe4 Bf5 5 Qe1! Bxb1 6 Bd2 Bd3 7 Bxa5 Qd7 8 Bc3. **2 Ne2 Nxe4! 3 Qxe4 Bf5 4 Qh4 Bxb1 5 Bg5 Bxa2 6 Bxe7 Qd7 7 Ng5 h6 8 Ne4 g5 9 Bxg5 hxg5 10 Nxg5 Rfe8** with a material preponderance coupled with adequate defenses to weather the attack.

172. Evans—Hesse, U.S. Championship 1948. (See Diagram 135 (p. 160).) Taboo is **1 e4? dxe4 2 fxe4 Nxe4! 3 Qxe4 Re8** winning by pinning. White trails in development and played **1 e3** hoping to harvest his two bishops by slowly preparing e4 after castling and swinging his rooks to the center.

173. Evans—R. Byrne, U.S. Open 1946. (See Diagram 112 (p. 134).) No! The knights look so menacing that White needlessly sacrificed the Exchange and lost with 1 Rxe5? Rxe5 1 Qxd4 Qc7. Better is **1 Qe3!** To exploit the draft around Black's king. It's still a hard fight after 1...**Ne4 2 Rd3 c5 3 Ne2.**

174. Evans—Reshevsky, U.S. Open 1955. (See Diagram 107 (p. 129).) In this Queen's Gambit Declined **1...exd5** is the correct recapture on the principle of freeing the "problem child" at c8. If **1...Nxd5 2 e4** gains a tempo by attacking the knight. On **1...Qxd5 2 Nc3 Bb4** Black must either lose a tempo by moving his queen again or permit White a spatial advantage after **3 Bd2 Bxc3 4 Bxc3 Ne4 5 e3 0-0 6 Bd3 Nxc3 7 bxc3 Nd7 8 0-0.**

175. Gassen—Evans, Marshall Club Championship 1946-47. (See Diagram 41 (p. 62).) White's pawns on d4 and c4 are technically known as "hanging pawns." They are in a state of flux—mobile yet not mobile at the same time. The game continued **1...Na5!** on the principle of piling up on the target at c4. **2 Ne5 Bxg2 3 Kxg2 Qa6** followed by Rac8 turning up the heat against the weak pawn at c4 (not to mention the pawn at a3).

176. Pilnick—Evans, U.S. Open 1952. (See Diagram 37 (p. 58).) Black has the better game because White is tied down to the defense of his backward c-pawn. Black also controls the c-file with an unassailable outpost on c4.

QUIZ

177. Evans—Larsen, U.S. Open 1949. (See Diagram 22 (p. 46).) White prepared a steamroller in the center with **1 Ra2!** intending Re2 followed by e4.

178. Evans—Carlyle, U.S. Open 1952. (See Diagram 22 (p. 46).) Against this Dutch Defense formation White must try to crack open the center with e4 hoping the backward pawn on e6 will become a target on the open e-file. The game continued: **1 f3! Qe8 2 e4** with initiative.

179. Evans—Maccioni, Dubrovnik Olympiad 1950. (See Diagrams 22 (p. 46), 23 (p. 47).) Anyone in his right mind can see that Black controls e4 four times and White only three times, so therefore 1 e4 is unplayable. But thanks to a tactical nuance, a wrong mind is needed.. The game continued: **1 e4! dxe4 2 fxe4 Bxe4 3 Rxf6! Bxg2 4 Rxd6!** The rook is lost anyway and "sells its life as dearly as possible" is the quant way Nimzovich would put it. Euwe calls this maneuver a "desperado theme." **Qxd6 5 Kxg2.** White nabbed two pieces for a rook and pawn, eventually winning, but it's still a hard fight.

180. Evans—Marro, Marshall Club Junior Championship 1947. (See Diagram 42 (p. 63).) Certainly White should take *en passant* on the principle of opening lines against a backward e-pawn. The game continued: **1 exf6! Bxf6 2 f4!** To stop ...e5 for good. **a5 3 Bh3 Nc7 4 Nef3** with a lasting bind.

181. Evans—Hudson, Intercollegiate Team Tournament 1950. (See Diagram 106 (p. 128).) Black's last move is inferior because it doesn't exert enough pressure on the center and lets White expand without putting up a fight. The game continued: **1 e4! Bb7 2 f3.** Getting cold feet. A good alternative is 3 e5 Ne4 4 Nxe4 Bxe4 5 Ne2. **d6 3 Nge2.** More logical is 3 Bd3 to develop the bishop first. **Nbd7 4 Be3 Be7 5 g3 e5 6 d5.** Black remains cramped.

182. Evans—Mednis, U.S. Open 1954. (See Diagram 141 (p. 166).) An interpolation that shatters Black is **1 b6!** Note that the prosaic 1 Qxb4? b6 gives Black a chance to consolidate. **cxb6 2 Nxb7 Qb8 3 Nxd8** winning the Exchange and the game came tumbling after.

183. Hans—Evans, match 1946. (See Diagram 108 (p. 130).) This Queen's Indian Defense is a struggle for control of the center which revolves around e4. If **1 0-0 Ne4!** followed by f5 claims squatter's rights on e4. Therefore more accurate is **1 Qc2!** on the principle of restriction or "prophylaxis."

184. Burger—Evans, U. S. Open 1952. (See Diagrams 79, 80, 81(p. 101-p. 103).) Correct is **1...Bf8!** on the principle of preserving two bishops in the endgame. Take only half credit for 1...Bh6 2 Be3 Bg7 4 Bd4 repeating moves when Black still must decide how to avoid swapping bishops. The game continued: **2 Ne3 Be6 3 a5 f5 4 g3 Bh6 5 Re2 f4 6 gxf4 Bxf4** with initiative.

185. Fink—Evans, U.S. Open 1953. (See Diagram 111 (p. 133).) **1...a5.** This secures the outpost on c5 by stopping b4 but cedes White a huge Space advantage with **2 e4!** No! If only for its nuisance value **1...e4** must be played! It weakens the Pawn Structure but implants a thorn in White's center. Black must calculate that the pawn will be safe on e4 before embarking on such a double-edge push, The game continued: **2 Ne1.** Better is 2 Nd4 a5. Weaker is 2 Ng5 Qe7 3 Rb1 a5. Or 2 Nd2 Bg4 3 Qe1 Re8 4 b4 Nd3! 5 Bxd3 exd3 6 Bb2 c6! with initiative. **a5.** Just in the nick of time to stop b4. **3 Na4?! Nxa4 4 Bxa4 Ng4! 5 h3 Ne5 6 Qe2 Qh4 7 Bd1 h5** with a fierce attack.

APPROACHING THE OPENING

"Chess is a sea in which a gnat may drink and an elephant may bathe."

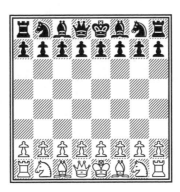

Diagram 186

"A complicated position."—Breyer

EVALUATION

Evaluation helps us navigate through a sea of complications. The process requires us to juggle various elements and weigh them against each other to decide who stands better. The crudest method is to count pieces to see who has more material, but if material is equal we're back to square one.

The starting lineup is symmetrical. With "best play" (whatever that is) the "perfect game" (whatever that is) should end in a draw. This is an ethical demand rather than a mathematical certainty. *"When evenly matched opponents play correctly, the games seldom have any content and frequently end in draws,"* Lasker stated. In other words, don't make a mistake and you can't lose! If neither side has a distinct advantage in Force, Space, Time or Pawn Structure, the probable outcome is a draw.

"Balanced positions with best play on either side must lead again and again to balanced positions," is another Lasker axiom. But keep in mind that there is no real equilibrium because chess is dynamic, in a constant state of flux, and a single move can alter the entire landscape.

Lasker invariably praised the man he trounced for the world championship in 1894: *"Steinitz elevates himself to the level of a genuine philosopher in demanding that the player with an advantage must attack with intent to win or else be punished by being deprived of his advantage."* From this it follows that the converse is true: A player who forces the issue without having an advantage must be prepared to pay the ultimate penalty—defeat.

Steinitz had the self-discipline and objectivity to evaluate each position as though he himself were not personally involved. He realized the master needs a killer instinct, but he also perceived that the mere will-to-win by itself isn't enough to secure victory. Alekhine's games, on the other hand, are characterized by sheer will, a fierce attempt to exert mind over matter.

APPROACHING THE OPENING

RUBINSTEIN—LASKER

St. Petersburg 1909

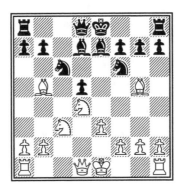

Diagram 187

White moves. The choice is between Force or Time. Many players would choose Time with **1 0-0** to pursue development and exert slow, steady pre;ssure on the isolani at d5. Not Rubinstein. He plays to win a pawn right away even though he must submit to an apparently irresistible attack. A plausible continuation is **1 0-0 a6 2 Be2 0-0 3 Bxf6.** No win of a pawn is in sight after 3 Rc1 Rc8 4 Bf3 Be6. **Bxf6 4 Nxd5 Bxd4 5 exd4 Be6** regaining the pawn with equality.

According to Reti in *Masters of the Chessboard,* if Rubinstein failed to take the pawn he would cease to heed that inner ethical voice, cease to be that humble and submissive player who trusted in his own judgment telling him that despite the pitfalls he can snatch the pawn and get away with it, that if he doesn't exercise his advantage right now it might evaporate. In the end Rubinstein did take the pawn —with fear and trembling, to be sure—yet confident that what is right must prevail.

The game continued: **1 Bxf6 Bxf6 2 Nxd5 Bxd4 3 exd4 Qg5.** Not 3...Qa5+ 4 Qd2 Qxb5? 5 Nc7+ forking the queen. **4 Bxc6.** Much too risky is 4 Nc7+ Kd8 5 Nxa8 Qxb5. **Bxc6**

203

5 Ne3 0-0-0 6 0-0 Rh8 7 Rc1 Rxe3 8 Rxc6+ bxc6 9 Qc1!
This is the miracle. Through this move, and only this move, White keeps his extra pawn and nurses it to an endgame which is handled with chiselled perfection. **Rxd4 10 fxe3 Rd7 11 Qxc6+ Kd8 12 Rf4!** White soon traded queens and won the rook and pawn ending. If 12...Rd1+ 13 Kf2 Rd2+ 14 Ke1 Qxg2 15 Rd4+ Rxd4 16 Qxg2 is the quietus.

IS THE FIRST MOVE AN ADVANTAGE?

W.F. Streeter wrote an article under the above heading in the May 1946 *Chess Review* summarizing the results by color of 5,598 games played in 45 tournaments between 1851-1932. His conclusions follow:

YEARS	WHITE WON	BLACK WON	DRAWN
1851–1878	46%	40%	14%
1881–1914	37%	31%	32%
1914–1932	37%	26%	37%
TOTAL	**38%**	**31%**	**31%**

Since then it has become much harder to win with Black and much easier to draw. In the 1920s Capablanca feared that chess would someday be played out. He predicted its "draw death" and in 1930 wrote an article proposing a 100-square board with two new pieces added for each side. Most games in grandmaster events today are drawn, alas, spurring experiments to change the rules, ban draw offers, speed up the clock, and alter the scoring system. I doubt that chess will ever die, but who knows what the future will bring?

MASTER PRACTICE

The way theoreticians evaluate openings is to examine the outcome of master games in which this opening is adopted. Manuals are crammed with statistical analysis of each variation and computers performing this function have largely usurped the role of humans. Meanwhile words are being displaced by fractions and symbols such as ++ to indicate who is winning. Let's examine a specific position and discuss the traditional approach.

Diagram 188

White moves—who stands better? This position in the Ruy Lopez was thought to be equal until 1954 when Geller found a sly interpolation. The first thing we notice is that White is on move and has the initiative. We must restrain our impulse to grab a piece by **1 Rxe4??** as soon as we see that **1...Rd1** mates. Normal moves like **1 Bf4** lead to naught after **1...Nc5** followed by Ne6 with a likely draw due to the balanced Pawn Structure (3 vs. 3 on each wing).

One thing is clear: White must exploit his Time advantage right now or lose it. If he can connect rooks by getting the bishop out of the way, then he can safely play Rxe4. Geller's sharp **1 Bh6!** fits this prescription. If **1...gxh6 2 Rxe4 Kf8 3 Rae1** leads to a winning endgame. Formula: Time transformed into Pawn Structure.

The tactical justification of **1 Bh6!** lies in two possibilities with Black's "desperado" knight. A desperado is a piece that's lost anyway, in exchange for which a player tries to get as much compensation as possible (see Diagram 179). The first variation is **1 Bh6! Nxc3 2 Bxg7 Rg8 3 Nxf7 Kxf7 4 Bxc3.** White extra pawn is decisive. Formula: Time into Force.

At this point the chess world condemned this position for Black, and the moves leading up to it were abandoned. But a second possibility must be examined before giving up. **1 Bh6! Nxf2 2 Bxg7 Rg8 3 Bf6! Nh3+.** Trickier is 3...Rd2!? 4 Kf1! Bxf6 5 Nc4+ and Nxd2. **4 Kf1 Bxf6 5 Nc6+ Kd7 6 Nxd8 Bxd8 7 Rad1+ Kc6 8 gxh3.** White's material superiority will prevail.

Geller's innovation is decisive, thus refuting the original verdict of equality, and hard analysis confirms that White wins. Previously we discussed **Time** (initiative is a sub-head) **Force, Space, Pawn Structure.** From this it follows that any position can be dissected into its component elements and then evaluated accordingly.

The concept which theoreticians accord primacy is master practice or past experience with a given position, just like precedents are cited in law books. It's hard to divorce theory from practice. We can't say, for instance, that White stands better in a certain position even though he lost every tournament game continuing from this position. If that's the case, then there's something wrong with the original evaluation.

Chess critics provide a court of last resort. But often they're guilty of the subjective fallacy and let reputations or the outcome of dubious games sway their judgment. Now this function is entrusted to computers.

A lot of analysis published in the pre-computer age is rubbish. For the most part Alekhine's work stands the test of time, yet there is the odd glitch. In his excellent tournament book of New York 1924 the great man stumbles when annotating Reti-Tartakower after **1 Nf3 g6 2 e4 c5 3 d4 cxd4 4 Nxd4 Nf6 5 Nc3 d6 7 Be2 Bg7 7 0-0 Nc6 8 Be3.** Alekhine writes: "More cautious is 8 h3, for now Black can play ...Ng4." But this simply costs a piece by 9 Bxg4 Bxg4 10 Nxc6 Bxd1 11 Nxd8 Bxc2 12 Nxb7, etc.

A bad move is a bad move whether it's suggested by a world champion or a duffer. Nothing can be accepted on blind faith. Taking a case at random, let's turn to *Modern Chess Openings* (8th edition). At the end of column 15 in the Slav Defense Alekhine's opinion is cited to the effect that "Black stands slightly better." But it turns out that the reverse is true.

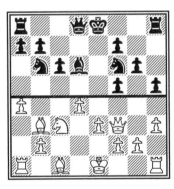

Diagram 189

WHITE MOVES—WHO STANDS BETTER?

The way to tackle this question is by examining each of the four elements in order to arrive at a conclusion.

> **Force:** Material is equal. White has the two bishops, an edge.
>
> **Space:** White has the freer game and **1 a5** would cramp Black, but there is no rush to push this pawn.

Time: Each side has three pieces developed and is ready to castle in one move. But since White is on move he has the initiative. White has two possible points of breakthrough—e4 or g4—as well as an option to breach the queenside with a5-a6.

Pawn Structure: Black's doubled pawns are a liability.

Master Practice: None quoted, just Alekhine's opinion.

Thus it appears that White stands better in every way. In fact, Black is in big trouble after **1 g4!** That's not to say he can't turn the tables and win (of course he can) only that he should avoid this particular variation of the Slav Defense because other lines offer Black better chances.

Most evaluations are not so clear-cut. The gambit, for instance, poses the knotty problem of weighing Force against Time. Most gambits have been analyzed so extensively for centuries that theory can provide a court of last resort without fearing the wrath of future generations. Take the Evans Gambit: **1 e4 e5 2 Nf3 Nc6 3 Bc4 Bc5 4 b4!? Bxb4 5 c3 Ba5.**

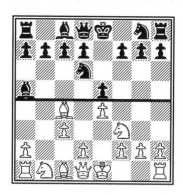

Diagram 190

Theory decrees that White has insufficient compensation for the pawn. This is true now and should be true 100 years from now despite "the light of later developments."

Nevertheless, many defenders never get out of the opening alive. A case in point is Fischer's 17 move shock victory in a skittles game against Reuben Fine (#44 in Fischer's *My 60 Memorable Games*).

Although the theoretical case against the Evans Gambit may be closed, there are three reasons why grandmasters still risk it against other grandmasters. (1) White has an improvement up his sleeve. (2) White rejects the traditional evaluation. (3) White knows it's inferior but counts on the element of surprise to carry the day. Of these three, the last is most likely—on the principle that fortune favors the brave.

Evaluation is not a prediction of result, it's merely an attempt to weigh dynamic elements at a given moment. An equal sign (=) means that neither side stands worse in the opinion of the writer. Equality doesn't mean the game should be drawn, only that the chances for both sides are delicately balanced. A massive amount of analysis has been lavished on openings for the simple reason that an early advantage is often decisive, despite Alekhine's boast that to lose he had to be beaten three times —once in the opening, once in the middle game, once in the ending.

THE FIRST MOVE

If we approach the opening without prejudice, there are some basic truths that we take for granted. We know that the center is of paramount importance, that pieces must be developed quickly, and that too many pawn moves can create weaknesses. This is a starting point.

A glance at the starting lineup reveals 20 possible moves—16 with the pawns and 4 with the knights. Which one is best? "It is astonishing how much hot water a master can wade into in the first dozen moves, despite a century of opening exploration," remarked Napier. The choice of a first move depends on personal preference and individual style.

As I write, I'm looking at the board with a completely open mind. It occurs to me that of these 20 moves perhaps only three are horrible: a4, h4, g4 because they create gaping, self-inflicted wounds in the Pawn Structure. They contribute nothing toward development, no threat, no contest for control of the center. Yet at the New York Tournament in 1880 Ware played **1...a5** each time he had Black, winning 4 and losing 5. With White he begin 2 games with **1 a4,** winning one and losing the other.

Two apparently useless knight moves—Nh3 and Na3— may be espoused by some Reti of the future. To the modern master who has been imbued with the principle of mobility these sorties seem outlandish and anti-positional. Yet there is a genuine concern that chess will be played out and that someday player may have to draw cards at random before each game to determine the opening (as in checkers). As early as 1868 a tournament was held in London where games began by reversing knights and bishops to avoid book lines. This is reminiscent of a proposal in the late 19th century that the United States close its patent bureau on the grounds that everything worthwhile already had been invented!

Yet there's still room for discovery and innovation in the opening. In fact, few masters have conquered all the intricacies of even one variation. At the 1933 Folkestone Olympiad, Arthur Dake defeated Hans Muller, the author of an authoritative treatise on the English Opening, in just 21 moves. The opening was an English Opening!

Nowadays many master games really begin after the first dozen or so moves instead of at move one. After Bobby Fischer won the world championship he became so disenchanted with what he dubbed the "old chess" that in the 1990s he touted Fischer Random or Chess 960 where each game must start from one of 960 possible positions chosen at random by machine. Ironically, he used computers to save chess from computers. Grandmaster tournaments already have been held with this variant, and more are expected in the future. Kasparov said most of these starting lineups are "poison to the eyes," yet Chess 960 or some other mutation could be the destiny of chess.

REVERSE OPENINGS

1 d4 or 1 e4 free two pieces (queen and bishop) and contest the center. Yet the moment a pawn advances two squares it creates an irretrievable weakness as well as a natural target. Once White has committed himself, Black then determines which tack the game will take. The idea behind reverse openings is that Black's defenses are so good that surely they must be even better if White adopts them with a move-in-hand.

The logical choice is the King's Indian, a universal setup no matter what Black does. This fianchetto has proved itself as a resilient and successful weapon for the second player. Curiously enough, there is no way to prevent White from setting it up with his eyes closed—ideal for someone who doesn't want to spend his life memorizing a bunch of book lines. (This is the essential theme of my book *The Chess Opening For You*.)

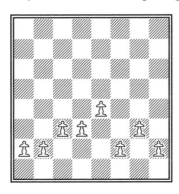

Diagram 191

White has a hole at d3 which is offset by his ability to maneuver behind closed lines. His weak light square complex (f3 and h3) is negligible as long as the bishop is retained on g2. Often the a-pawn is pushed to a4 so that a knight on c4 can't be dislodged by ...b5.

After either **1 e4** or **1 Nf3** White can channel the game into a reverse King's Indian against almost anything Black does. Thus in the French Defense **1 e4 e6 2 d3** produces the desired result.

Diagram 192

The game might continue with **2...d5 3 Nd2 Nf6 4 g3 Be7 5 Bg2 0-0 6 Ngf3 c5 7 0-0 Nc6** which are all logical moves.

Diagram 193

Exactly the same position was reached by transposition in Evans—Sherwin, New York 1955: **1 Nf3 Nf6 2 g3 d5 3 g3 d5 4 Bg2 e6 5 d3 0-0 6 Nbd2 c5 7 e4 Nc6.** Voilà! To show how quickly White can whip up an attack, here's the entire game: **8 c3 Rb8 9 Re1 Re8 10 e5 Nd7 11 Nf1 b5 12 h4 a5 13 Bf4 Ba6 14 N1h2 Qc7 15 h5 b4 16 Ng4 a4 17 c4 dxc4 18 dxc4 Bxc4 19 Qxa4 Nb6 20 Qc2 b3 21 axb3 Nb4 22 Qc3 N4d5 23 Qc1 Bxb3 24 Bg5 Nb4 25 Re3 Bd5 26 h6 g6 27 Rea3 Nc4 28 Bxe7 Rxe7 29 Qf4 Qd8 30 Nf6+ Kh8 31 Nxh7 Rc7 32 Nhg5 Qe7 33 Ra7 Rxa7 34.Rxa7 Rb7 35 Ra8+ 1–0**

It's apparent that White's passive setup conceals much attacking potential, and transpositions are abundant. Reshevsky-Botvinnik, Moscow 1955 began: **1 e4 e6 2 d3 c5 3 g3 Nc6 4 Bg2 g6 5 Nd2 Bg7 6 Ngf3 Nge7 7 0-0 0-0 8 Re1 d6 9 c3 h6 10 Nb3 e5 11 d4 b6** with equal chances. This could also arise from the Sicilian Defense after **1 e4 c5 2 d3 e6.**

The element of Time is not so critical in closed positions as in open ones. By adopting these reverse openings White postpones a sharp, early struggle, until the middle game. The King's Indian Reversed used to be a pet opening of the youthful Bobby Fischer who gave it up because it didn't offer White enough of an initiative. If Black maintains the symmetry by copying White's moves, the game often assumes a drawish character.

SYMMETRICAL POSITIONS

The starting lineup is symmetrical. After making his first move White disrupts the harmony. Black can copy—but not for long. Petrov's Defense illustrates the point: **1 e4 e5 2 Nf3 Nf6 3 Nxe5 Nxe4?** Correct is 3...d6 4 Nf3 Nxe4) **4 Qe2 d5 5 d3 Qe7.** Not 5...Nf6?? 6 Nc6+. **6 dxe4 Qxe5 7 exd5** gaining a pawn with a winning endgame.

In reverse openings, however, Black can copy for a very long time. Take a look at Evans—Lombardy, New York 1956: **1 Nf3 Nf6 2 g3 g6 3 Bg2 Bg7 4 0–0 0–0 5 d3 d6 6 c4 c5 7 Nc3 Nc6 8 Bd2 Rb8 9 a3 a6 10 Rb1 b5 11 cxb5 axb5 12 b4 cxb4 13 axb4 Bd7 14 h3 h6.**

HELLO SYMMETRY

Diagram 194

If White has an advantage, it is indeed very slight and the course of the game bears this out: **15 e4 Ne8 16 Nd5 Nc7 17 Nxc7 Qxc7 18 d4 e5 19 Qc1 Qc8 20 Bxh6 Nxd4 21 Nxd4**

Qxc1 22 Bxc1 exd4 23 Rd1 Rfc8 24 Bb2 Rc4 25 Ba1 Bc6 26 f3 d5 27 Bf1 Rc2 28 Bxd4 dxe4 29 Bxg7 Kxg7 30 Rbc1 Rxc1 31 Rxc1 Rb6 32 fxe4 Bxe4 33 Rc5 Bc6. It was soon drawn.

The symmetrical defense puts the Queen's Gambit to a severe test after **1 d4 d5 2 c4 c5!?** Can White preserve the initiative?

Diagram 195

Evans—Bisguier, New York 1955 continued: **3 cxd5 Nf6 4 Nf3 cxd4 5 Qxd4 Qxd5 6 Nc3 Qa5** followed by Nc6 regaining the lost tempo and White got almost nothing out of the opening. The best way to stay on top is **3 dxc5! e6 4 cxd5 exd5 5 Be3** (or 5 Nc3 d4 6 Na4).

In the hands of a master technician the advantage of the move is often decisive in symmetrical positions. Witness the following mirror image in Reshevsky (New York)—Stahlberg (Argentina) in a 1947 radio match where White seems to make something out of nothing

Diagram 196
White moves

1 Bg5! Re8 2 Rac1 h6 3 Be3 Bf5 4 Rc7 Bxd3? This seems wrong on principle. Better is 4...Bg4! Now White's two bishops rake the board. **5 exd3 Rac8 6 Rfc1 Rxc7 7 Rxc7 Bxb2 8 Bxb7 Bf6.** Hoping for 9 Bxa7? Nb5! No such luck! **9 Bc6 Rb8 10 Bxa7 Rb1+ 11 Kg2 Ra1 12 a4 Nf5 13 Bb6 Bd4 14 a5 Bc3 15 Ra7 Nd4 16 Be3 Nb3 17 a6 Bd4 18 Bxd4 Nxd4 19 Rd7 f5 20 Bd5+ 1-0.**

SUMMING UP

This book tackles the practical question of how you can radically improve by applying basic principles to your own games. My approach has been to break chess down into four components: Pawn Structure, Space, Force and Time. The order is somewhat arbitrary, though Pawn Structure comes first because it is the most difficult concept to grasp. A realization that the pawn is "the soul of chess" is prerequisite to further analysis of other elements.

In chemical terms Pawn Structure and Force are inert, whereas Space and Time are volatile. Broadly speaking, an advantage in the inert (or stable) elements manifests itself most decisively in the endgame. An advantage in the volatile (or unstable) elements is far more crucial in the opening where rapid development and central control are transcendent.

In the middle game, if material is equal, Time and Space have a tendency to predominate. A quick decision in the early stages of the game is unlikely between equally matched opponents. Hence victory is possible only after someone errs. When the minor advantages which accrue are exploited with precision we call it "good technique." The problem is how to win by converting the volatile into the inert elements. The bulk of this book features practical examples taken mostly from my tournament games.

STABLE ELEMENTS

Pawn Structure is akin to bone structure. Since a pawn is the only unit that can never retreat, it should be pushed sparingly. A hasty weakness seldom can be repaired. The unique power of the pawn to queen when it reaches the eighth rank alters the dynamics of endgame strategy and elevates this foot soldier to regal significance.

An advantage in Force is decisive if all other things are equal. The gain of even a single pawn in the opening is usually fatal between masters. To be ahead in material is to be wealthier than your opponent. Hence swapping pieces is the pattern for covering Force into victory.

UNSTABLE ELEMENTS

A space advantage means superior mobility, more elbow room to maneuver and fluid lines of communication. Cramped positions, as Dr. Tarrasch observed, bear the germs of defeat. In order to break his shackles a player often must make grave concessions in Force or Pawn Structure. Then it becomes a matter of enforcing the task of winning a won game, which is often the hardest thing to do in chess. "I had a won game!" moaned many a player after tipping over his king.

An advantage in Time confers the initiative. Pieces that are centralized and well-developed are ready to strike deeply into enemy terrain. It bears repeating that tempo is so crucial that a mediocre player could become world champion if granted the right to move twice in a row each game.

BRIEF OVERVIEW

In Chapter One we reviewed the turmoil among Romantics, Classicists, Hypermoderns, Technicians and Tacticians. We saw that chess sways between art and science just like Muhammed's coffin sways between heaven and earth.

Chess is a competitive struggle between two minds within a mechanistic framework. Lasker saw it as a clash of wills in which the rounded person and not necessarily the better player was bound to prevail. Norbert Wiener, a pioneer in cybernetics, envisaged a future where machines "might be as good as the vast majority of the human race." Nowadays machines have exceeded his wildest dreams. Not only can they find the best move in a split second, they also routinely defeat the top players.

The American school of chess has been described as pragmatic because it reflects the culture. The Soviet school has been called dynamic because it seems to be based on counterattack rather than attack. A noted psychologist hinted that this style of play mirrors a social structure where individual initiative is reduced to a minimum. Frankly, these speculations should be taken with a grain of salt. I think that W.C. Fields got it right when he quipped: *"Ultimately chess is just chess. Not the best thing in the world and not the worst thing in the world, but there is nothing quite like it."*

Pragmatism as a method or way of life becomes odious only when its adherents worship at the fount of success or make the smug deduction that a certain course of action is "best because it works." The principles advocated in this book work because they are best, the distilled heritage of centuries of chess evolution. As Lasker noted, hypocrisy and error don't survive for long on the chessboard—the merciless fact culminates in checkmate and contradicts the hypocrite.

The preceding chapters form an organic whole by demonstrating the basic principles which guide my play in theory and practice. This book contains all my "secrets" and might have saved me a year of groping in the dark if someone had set them down for me in black and white when I first started.

Chess is a universal language belonging to all nations that has travelled without passport throughout the ages. As Stefan Zweig put it, nobody knows the divinity who bestowed it upon the world to slay boredom, sharpen the wits and exhilarate the spirit.

The chessboard is a place of joy, stimulation and intellectual challenge. There is beauty there. And truth.

BIBLIOGRAPHY

Alekhine, A. *My Best Games of Chess.* In 2 volumes. Harcourt, Brace & Co., New York, 1939.

Chernev, I. *Winning Chess Traps. Chess Review,* New York, 1946.

Du Mont, J. *The Basis of Coimbination in Chess.* George Routledge & Sons, Ltd., London, 1946.

Euwe, M. *Meet the Masters.* Sir Isaac Pitman & Sons, Ltd., London, 1945.

Euwe, M. *Strategy and Tactics in Chess.* David McKay Co., Philadelphia, 1937.

Evans L. *Trophy Chess.* Charles Scribner & Sons, New York, 1956.

Fine, R. *Basic Chess Endings.* David McKay Co., Philadelphia, 1941.

Fine, R. *The Ideas Behind the Chess Openings.* David McKay Co., Philadelphia, 1943.

Kmoch, H. *Rubinstein's Chess Masterpieces.* Horowitz & Harkness, New York, 1941.

König, I. *Chess from Morphy to Botvinnik.* G. Bell & Sons, Ltd., London, 1951.

Korn, W. and Evans, L. *Modern Chess Openings.* Tenth Edition. Pitman Publishing Corporation, New York 1965.

Lasker, Em. *Manual of Chess.* David McKay Co., Philadelphia, 1947.

Nimzovitch, A. *My System.* David McKay Co., Philadelphia, 1947.

Reinfeld, F. *Keres' Best Games of Chess.* David McKay Co., Philadelphia, 1942.

Reinfeld, F. *Practical End-Game Play.* David McKay Co., Philadelphia, 1949.

Reinfeld, F. *The Immortal Games of Capablanca.* Pitman Publishing Corporation, New York 1942.

Reinfeld, F. and Chernev, I. *Chess Strategy and Tactics.* David McKay Co., Philadelphia, 1946.

Réti, R. *Masters of the Chessboard.* Whittlesey House, New York, 1932.

Réti, R. *Modern Ideas in Chess.* David McKay Co., Philadelphia, 1923.

Spielmann, R. *The Art of Sacrifice in Chess.* David McKay Co., Philadelphia, 1935.

Znosko-Borovsky, E. *The Middle Game in Chess.* David McKay Co., Philadelphia, 1946.

INDEX

INDEX